A Practical Guide to the Law in Relation to Migrant Victims of Domestic Violence

A Practical Guide to the Law in Relation to Migrant Victims of Domestic Violence

Priya Solanki

Barrister

Law Brief Publishing

Published 2024 by Law Brief Publishing, an imprint of Law Brief Publishing Ltd
30 The Parks
Minehead
Somerset
TA24 8BT

www.lawbriefpublishing.com

Paperback: 978-1-913715-94-6

Priya Solanki is a sought-after barrister practising at One Pump Court Chambers.

She has over 15 years' experience. She has an extensive practice in all areas of immigration (including business immigration), asylum, deportation, trafficking, unlawful detention and EUSS applications.

She regularly provides in-house training, seminars and webinars for Immigration Law Practitioners Association, Data Law and other organisations. She has delivered extensive training on the topic of domestic violence in immigration law, including on the extensive changes recently introduced by the MVDA and Appendix Victims of Domestic Abuse.

Priya also has a particular interest in and vast experience of cases involving gender-based violence and vulnerable clients. She is a popular choice for solicitors looking to instruct counsel in DV cases and is considered as creative in her approach to these claims.

Prior to coming to the Bar, Priya practised in immigration and asylum law as a supervisor and senior caseworker at a not-for-profit organisation. This gives her the great advantage of being able to assist with case preparation before cases reach appeal stage. This combined with her extensive advocacy experience makes her a popular choice for both clients and instructing solicitors.

She is ranked Leading Junior barrister in immigration by the Legal 500 and Chambers & Partners. The Directories state that "Priya is dedicated, highly committed, excellent with clients", "she has a passion for this area of work particularly in working for vulnerable survivors of domestic violence and trafficking", "she is very knowledgeable and responsive and her advocacy is fantastic" and "she is always up to speed with the latest legal developments and is very good at assisting with the strategy of cases before the litigation stage is reached."

Priya has been appointed as a Deputy Upper Tribunal Judge (Immigration and Asylum Chamber). Priya is also an Independent Funding Adjudicator for the Legal Aid Agency and the Co-Chair of the Legal Aid Agency Review Panel. She carries out these roles part-time alongside her work at the Bar.

My husband, Ritesh, and my children, Simran and Raj - thank you for always taking an interest in my work and supporting me every day.

To all of my wider family, but in particular Asha, Mum, Dad and Aruna - thank you for keeping me sane (and for the childcare which allowed me to write this book). And Ba and Bapuji, thank you for all your love.

Also, a huge thank you to my supportive colleagues at One Pump Court Chambers. In particular I thank, Ian Burrow, Mycal Thomas and James Rourke, for clerking me so wonderfully. Thanks also to my friend and wonderful instructing solicitor, Irene Tsherit, for her support in writing this book.

PREFACE

Statistics show that around 21% of adults experience domestic violence in their lifetime[1].

DV affects both men and women, with statistics showing that one third of DA victims are men, 13.9% of men are estimated to face DA in their lifetime[2].

Risks of violence for migrants are much higher. Domestic abuse rates amongst migrant females have been reported to be as high as 49.8%[3].

There are several barriers to victims of DV coming forward to report abuse; namely shame, embarrassment, residual love, wanting the relationship to work, fear and control, lack of understanding and knowledge of their circumstances. The obstacles facing immigration victims are greater as their visas depend upon their abusive partners and may have little or no knowledge of how the immigration system, with all of its complexities, works. A poll in 2017 carried out amongst organisations that worked with domestic violence survivors reported that 80% of migrant victims were scared to report their abuse to the police[4].

---

1 Office for National Statistics, Domestic Abuse in England and Wales Overview: November 2022; National Centre for Domestic Violence, Domestic Abuse Statistics UK 2022

2 Office for National Statistics, Domestic Abuse in England and Wales Overview: November 2022

3 National Organisation for Women, Intimate Partner Violence Documented and Immigrant Women, 2017

4 California Health Report, Facing Anti-Immigrant Rhetoric and ICE raids, Fewer Undocumented Victims Willing to Report Domestic Violence, Claudia Boyd-Barett, 21 February 2019

This book is essential reading for those working with migrant victims of domestic violence.

It will allow practitioners to advise their clients thoroughly in these matters and to make better evidenced applications. It will further allow for stronger challenges to decisions which refuse leave to victims of domestic violence.

The stated law in this book is believed to be correct and up-to-date to 1st August 2024.

Priya Solanki
August 2024

CONTENTS

CHAPTER ONE

THE DEFINITION OF DOMESTIC ABUSE

Over the years there have been changes and improvements to the definition of domestic violence. This has been to the benefit of clients.

In 2012 a new and broader definition of domestic was set out by the government in an attempt to further confront violence against women and girls[1]. This followed a recommendation from the Home Affairs Select Committee Report in 2008 to include victims under the age of 18[2], and a consultation launched in late 2011 to March 2012 which sought views (from local authorities, the police, the charitable and voluntary sector as well as many others) on the definition in place at that stage and the idea of expanding the same[3].

In 2021 the Domestic Abuse Act 2021 came into force. The 2021 Act had many goals and purposes. These included, for example, banning GPs for charging for medical evidence of domestic abuse, creating new criminal offences, and importantly for our purposes founding a legal definition of domestic abuse which recognised children as victims in their own right, and establishing a statutory definition of domestic abuse which emphasised that domestic abuse is not just physical violence.

---

1 Home Office News Story, New definition of domestic violence, 18 September 2012

2 Sixth Report From The Home Affairs Committee Session 2007-08 HC 263

3 Home Office, Cross-Government Definition of Domestic Violence – A Consultation Summary of Responses, September 2012

The definition of domestic violence, as set out in the Home Office Policy Guidance on Appendix Victim of Domestic Abuse ('AVDA Guidance')[4], is based on the legal definition of domestic abuse as set out in the Domestic Abuse Act 2021 (the 2021 Act). It is "any single incident or pattern of conduct where someone's behaviour towards another is abusive, and where the people involved are aged 16 or over and are, or have been, personally connected to each other (regardless of gender or sexuality)." It can be seen that there are several aspects to this definition.

The reference to personal connection, is described further in the s2(1) of the 2021 Act and the AVDA Guidance[5] as including where the individuals are married, civil partners, have been in an intimate personal relationship with each other, have been parents or had a parental relationship to the same child, or are relatives. Relatives is defined further in s2(3) of the 2021 Act and s63 of the Family Law Act 1996 as including in-laws and step-family. If an individual is able to show that their relationship has ended owing to abuse from a mother-in-law or extended family for example, they can qualify for settlement. The abuse must still be the reason for the relationship breaking down[6].

Whilst the definition above refers to those over the age of 16, practitioners will be aware that for the purpose of the immigration rules, a partner has to be over the age of 18 to qualify for leave as a partner. Importantly, the AVDA Guidance makes clear that where a relationship has broken down owing to a family member (such as a child) in a household being subjected to DA the abused partner can qualify for settlement. They may for example have ended their relationship or left the house in order to protect a child[7]. This is in accordance with s.1(5) of the 2021 Act which states that 'for the purposes of this Act [the

---

4 Version 17.0 dated 4 April 2024 at pp20-21

5 Ibid. p20

6 Ibid. p16

7 Ibid. p17

abuser's] behaviour may be behaviour "towards" [the victim] despite the fact that it consists of conduct directed at another person (for example, [the victim's child).' Further, s3(2) of the Domestic Abuse Act 2021 says that 'any reference in this Act to a victim of domestic abuse includes a reference to a child who— (a) sees or hears, or experiences the effects of, the abuse, and (b)is related to [the abuser] or [the victim].' We will revisit the issue of child victims later in this title.

Abusive behaviour is defined in s.1(3) of the 2021 Act as physical abuse, sexual abuse, violent behaviour, threatening behaviour, controlling behaviour, coercive behaviour, financial abuse, psychological abuse, emotional abuse and other abuse. We will look at the different types of abusive behaviour in more detail below.

s.1(4) of the 2021 Act defines financial abuse as conduct which affects an individual's ability to acquire money, use money, maintain money or other property, or the inability to obtain goods or services.

Controlling behaviour is 'a range of acts designed to make a person subordinate or dependent by isolating them from sources of support, exploiting their resources and capacities for personal gain, depriving them of the means needed for independence, resistance and escape, regulating their everyday behaviour[8]. This is further broken down in the Home Office Statutory Guidance[9] as, for example, using digital systems such as smart devices or social media to monitor or upset the victim (e.g., using location tracking, checking phone use), controlling daily activities (dictating what they wear, eat, where they sleep, who they speak to), directing their spending and accounts and benefits, denying access to

---

8 Home Office Policy Guidance on Appendix Victim of Domestic Abuse, Version 17.0 04 April 2024, p20

9 Controlling or Coercive Behaviour: Statutory Guidance Framework, 5 April 2023, p15

their work or turning up at their work, following them, and/or using substances to direct an individual.

Coercive behaviour is described as 'an act or a pattern of acts of assault, threats, humiliation and intimidation'[10]. Again Statutory Guidance helpfully breaks this down further as for example making accusations in public or private for deviating from the rules of their household/relationship, making false allegations, intimidations to go to the police, threatening the person to carry out criminal behaviour, threats to expose sensitive information (e.g., health status, sexual activity, sexual orientation), threatening precarious immigration status[11].

The AVDA Guidance makes clear that DA includes 'honour' based violence, female genital mutilation (FGM), forced marriage, dowry-related abuse and transnational marriage abandonment.

The Domestic Abuse Statutory Guidance sets out that 'honour-based abuse is a crime or incident which has or may have been committed to protect or defend the perceived honour of the family and/or community, or in response to individuals trying to break away from constraining 'norms' of behaviour that their family or community is trying to impose.'[12]

FGM is also referred to as female cutting, female circumcision, when the genitals of a female are changed or removed on purpose for reasons which are not medical[13].

---

10 Home Office Policy Guidance on Appendix Victim of Domestic Abuse, Version 17.0 04 April 2024, p20

11 Domestic Abuse Statutory Guidance July 2022 pp31-32; Controlling or Coercive Behaviour: Statutory Guidance Framework, 5 April 2023 pp15-16

12 July 2022, pp42-43

13 s.1 Female Genital Mutilation Act 2003

Dowry involves money or gifts or property being handed from the bride's family to the in-laws or groom prior to or during or after a marriage. It has been suggested by the U.N. Division for the Advancement of Women that dowry related abuse occurs when there is any act of violence or harassment associated with the giving or receiving of dowry[14].

Forced marriage involves the use of violence, threats or any other form of coercion for the purpose of causing another person to enter into a marriage, where the person believes, or ought reasonably to believe, that the conduct may cause the other person to enter into the marriage without free and full consent[15].

TMA is where a migrant victim of DA is abandoned overseas, by their spouse or partner, against their will and usually with the goal of preventing them from returning to the UK[16]. There is a chapter dedicated to TMA in this book and we will look further at the definition there.

Practitioners should have regard to this very extensive definition when advising clients, who may well not understand that being isolated or humiliated for example amounts to violence, and when preparing and gathering evidence for the applications that we discuss further on in this book.

---

14 Good Practices in Legislation on "Harmful Practices" Against Women United Nations Division for the Advancement of Women United Nations Economic Commission for Africa Addis Ababa, Ethiopia, 26 to 29 May 2009, p20

15 s.121 Anti-social Behaviour, Crime and Policing Act 2014

16 Home Office Policy Guidance on Appendix Victim of Domestic Abuse, Version 17.0 04 April 2024, p23

CHAPTER TWO

SEEKING LEAVE UNDER THE MIGRANT VICTIMS OF DOMESTIC ABUSE CONCESSION

Individuals who are in the UK on a spouse or partner visa usually have a condition attached to their leave which says No Recourse to Public Funds ('NRPF'). As many victims are controlled, isolated, financially abused, have no bank accounts, do not work, have never worked and may have no work experience or qualifications, the NRPF condition can prevent them from fleeing domestic abuse. The fact that they are prevented from applying for benefits or having access to a refuge or safe housing, means they have no choice but to rely on their abusive partner.

In 2009 the Sojourner Project Pilot Scheme was launched. This scheme gave migrant victims of DV, with the NRPF condition attached to their leave, access to housing and subsistence costs for 40 days whilst their applications for settlement as victims of DV were considered. This enabled them to flee their matrimonial home. Between 2009 and 2011 the Sojourner Project helped 1,522 individuals[17].

It was however appreciated that a long-term solution needed to be put into place to address this problem. It was noted that many victims were not able to gather evidence and make domestic violence applications within that short period of time, some could not locate legal aid solicitors in that timescale. Even where an application could be made in the

---

17 News story, Home Office and The Rt Hon Damian Green MP, Support for Victims of Domestic Violence, 2 April 2012

permitted timeframe, decisions often took longer and where refused there was no subsistence or housing available for victims during an appeal[18] (NB: appeal rights were different at that stage to those in place now; which is a matter discussed in Chapter 8 of this book).

On 1 April 2012 the Destitution Domestic Violence Concession (DDVC) was introduced[19]. This allowed a migrant victim of DV, who was eligible to make an application for Indefinite Leave to Remain ('ILR')/settlement, to inform the Home Office that they needed access to public funds to make their DV settlement application. It allowed an individual to seek leave outside the immigration rules ('LOTR'), without any condition preventing access to public funds being applied to their leave. It created a grant of LOTR for a period of 3 months. Once the LOTR was granted, it allowed the migrant victim to claim benefits and have access to safe accommodation whilst they sought legal representation, gathered evidence of DA from GPs or for example the police of DV, and made an application for ILR based on DV. The leave, and the conditions attached to the LOTR, continued whilst the ILR application was outstanding with the Home Office and whilst a victim made an in-time administrative review challenge against any adverse decision made by the UK Visas and Immigration ('UKVI').

On 16 February 2024 the Home Office published changes to the DDVC. The concession is now called the Migrant Victims of Domestic Abuse Concession (MVDAC). It is set out in Home Office Policy, namely Migrant Victims of Domestic Abuse Concession (formerly the destitute domestic violence concession (DDVC)) Version 4.0 04 April 2024 ('MVDAC Policy').

---

18 Home Affairs Committee Eight Report Forced Marriage, Written evidence submitted by Southall Black Sisters, March 2011

19 See the now archived Home Office Guidance, Destitute Domestic Violence (DDV) Concession Version 1.0 05 February 2018

The MVDAC does not negatively change rights or benefits under the DDVC. Those eligible under the DDVC remain eligible under MVDAC. The MVDAC also continues to assist DA victims in the same way as the DDVC did. It provides 3 months LOTR to migrant victims whose relationship has broken down as a result of DV, where they hold leave as a partner in the right category[20], where they require leave independent from their partner and want to have the option to apply for public funds to seek the same if they have the correct immigration status to make an application. In addition to access to public funds, those granted LOTR are allowed to work and study.

It is important to be aware that it is not just the NRPF condition that may necessitate an application under MVDAC. Practitioners may be aware that for many it is for many necessary to tell the Home Office when they separate or divorce if their leave is dependent on their relationship with their partner[21]. The MVDAC allows applicants to inform the Home Office of the breakdown (where it is caused by DV) and apply for a short period of leave whilst they prepare any further application.

Positively, the MVDAC is broader in respect of eligibility than the DDVC. Whilst the DDVC only allowed victims who qualified for settlement as a victim of DV to apply, the new concession also allows for a dependent partner of a migrant on a student or work route to also seek LOTR for a period of 3 months. This allows these victims to flee their violent relationship and to further have recourse to public funds.

---

20 Please note victims that hold or held leave that meets the requirements of VDA 4.1(a)-(f) will be eligible under MVDAC as well as some extended categories that are provided for in the MVDAC and as explained in this Chapter.

21 See Immigration Rule 9.23.1, and Home Office Policy Guidance, Cancellation and Curtailment of Permission Version 5.0 05 March 2024 p70 and https://www.gov.uk/visas-when-you-separate-or-divorce

This extension in policy is said by the Home Office to be in response to the Support for Migrant Victims ('SMV') Scheme which ran as a pilot between 2021 and 2022 to support migrant victims of DA and their children who were subject to the NRPF condition[22].

Practitioners will be pleased to learn that work route is also defined broadly in the MVDAC Policy. It is said that where a work route under the immigration rules allows for dependent partners to be given leave, those dependent partners will fall under the concession[23]. This includes for example dependent partners of those on a skilled worker visa, graduate visa, health and care worker visa, representative of an overseas business visa or on a secondment worker visa (global business mobility) amongst others[24].

It is however important to note that dependent partners of workers or students are not eligible to apply for settlement on the grounds of DV under the immigration rules, namely Appendix Victims of Domestic Abuse[25]. The concession states that these individuals can make an application for leave in another relevant route[26] (see for example in Chapter 7 of this title), or make plans to leave the UK after having received financial support and assistance from any specialist services[27]. It follows that applicants need to be advised with care; they must be

---

22 Home Office Research and analysis, Evaluating the support for Migrant Victims (SMV) Pilot: Findings from a process evaluation, 4 August 2023

23 Migrant Victims of Domestic Abuse Concession (formerly the destitute domestic violence concession (DDVC)) Version 4.0 04 April 2024 p7

24 See https://www.gov.uk/browse/visas-immigration/work-visas

25 Chapter 4 of this book looks at who is eligible to apply for ILR as a victim of DA. It is stressed that this is different to who is eligible to apply for the MVDA Concession.

26 They may have an protection claim, human rights claim or an application in another immigration route they can pursue.

27 See pp4-5.

informed that applying for the MVDAC will mean that their leave as a dependent partner may be cancelled[28] and varied permanently. These individuals should consider whether there is any application they could make with their existing leave that may be more beneficial to them than 3 months LOTR. If these migrant victims do not make a further application for leave before their 3 months LOTR expires, or if any further application they make thereafter is refused (without a right of appeal or they go on to exhaust any appeal rights against a refusal) they will become an overstayer and be liable to removal.

Dependent partners under the Hong Kong British National (Overseas) route cannot apply and do not need to apply under MVDAC. This is because they need not tell the UKVI if their relationship ends. This is because they have a route to settlement which is not dependent on their relationship with their partner[29] (see Appendix Hong Kong British National (Overseas)[30]). Please note that limited leave under the Hong Kong British National (Overseas) route is granted with NRPF. As such,

---

28 Home Office Policy Guidance, Cancellation and Curtailment of Permission Version 5.0 05 March 2024, pp70-78

29 Unfortunately, dependent partners and spouses on the Hong Kong British National (Overseas) route whose relationships break down owing to domestic violence do not qualify for settlement immediately on that basis (unlike those catered for in Appendix Victim of Domestic Violence). Instead they qualify for ILR in their own right under their route after they have completed five years of leave; see Appendix Hong Kong British National (Overseas) at HK 62.1-64.2; see Home Office Policy Guidance Appendix Hong Kong British National (Overseas) route Version 10.0 10 April 2024 at pp52-58

30 See also Home Office Policy Guidance, Cancellation and Curtailment of Permission Version 5.0 05 March 2024, p71

it may well be necessary to submit an application to have conditions of leave changed to have the NRPF lifted[31].

Further, individuals with pre-settled status under the EU Settlement Scheme as a partner need not inform the Home Office of the breakdown of their relationship as they can continue to qualify for leave under Appendix EU despite their relationship ending, and they do not have a NRPF condition attached to their status (though accessing public funds can be difficult for some with this status[32]). However, they are eligible to apply under MVDAC and applying under MVDAC may address any problems they are facing with accessing public funds. I discuss this category of individuals further later in this book.

Dependent children (aged under 18, or aged over 18 if last granted leave as a dependent child of the parent and not leading an independent life) can be included in the MVDAC application[33]. Again, children should be advised with care. The Guidance makes clear that a British child or settled child included in an application under MVDAC should be disregarded. Advisers should consider whether it may be more beneficial for a child to remain on the visa route they are currently on, whether the child's status or route to ILR may or may not be affected by the breakdown of the relationship, whether they may have an alternative route available to them for ILR, whether or not the child needs access to public funds, or whether the child would meet the requirements as a dependent under Appendix Victim of Domestic Abuse.

---

31 See Appendix Hong Kong British National (Overseas) at HK 65.1-65.3; UKVI Form Guidance on applying to change your permission, Updated 10 January 2024

32 When applying for benefits or housing those with pre-settled status have to meet a right to reside test; see *Secretary of State for Work and Pensions v AT* [2023] 2 W.L.R. 967

33 Migrant Victims of Domestic Abuse Concession (formerly the destitute domestic violence concession (DDVC)) Version 4.0 04 April 2024 p8

The application form to complete for the MVDAC concession is available online[34]. It is a free application. The completed form is to be sent either by post to Liverpool or by email to DomesticViolence2@homeoffice.gov.uk. Processing times will be longer for applications submitted by post.

The form asks for basic personal details of the Applicant such as name, nationality, address, contact details, spouse or partner details, Biometric Residence Permit (BRP) details, dependant's details and representative details. It asks basic questions such as, whether their relationship has broken down permanently owing to DA, whether they need leave independent of their partner, and whether they require access to public funds to support themselves and any dependent children in the UK.

If the individual qualifies for the LOTR they will be sent a letter confirming a grant of LOTR and issued a biometric residence permit ('BRP') with this status. The letter will advise them whether or not they can go on to make an application for ILR under Appendix Victim of Domestic Abuse.

The grant of LOTR does not result in automatic benefits; the applicant will need to make an application to the Department of Work and Pensions (DWP) for any benefits and there will be an assessment of what they are entitled to[35].

It is important to note that a grant of LOTR under the MVDAC does not guarantee that an applicant will qualify for ILR as a victim of DV. Eligibility for settlement will be considered under the immigration rules discussed later in this book. Where eligible to do so, an applicant must

---

https://assets.publishing.service.gov.uk/media/6602fbc6f1d3a09b1f32ad75/Form_for_migrant_victims_of_domestic_abuse_concession.pdf

35 See Home Office and DWP Guidance Help available from the Department for Work and Pensions for people who are victims of domestic violence and abuse 16 April 2014

make an application for settlement as a DV victim showing they meet the rules. They must do this within the three-month LOTR period. This will prevent them from becoming an overstayer and to ensure they continue to have leave under Section 3C of the Immigration Act 1971. It can of course be difficult to obtain medical records, police records, expert evidence etc., within this timescale. It may be important to advise the Home Office of any evidence that is outstanding when the application is being submitted, together with a timescale (and any evidence) of when it is expected. If an individual does not apply within the three months' timescale, they will become an overstayer.

The target time for dealing with a DA settlement application is 6 months[36], but it is not uncommon for decisions to take much longer.

Owing to the Immigration Act 2014[37], there is no right of appeal against a refusal of an application under the MVDAC. As explained in Chapter 8 of this book, there is now only a right of appeal against a decision to refuse a protection claim (refugee status or humanitarian protection) and a decision to refuse a human rights claim. The MVDAC Policy allows for a reconsideration to be requested where the policy has been applied incorrectly; any reconsideration has to be agreed by a senior caseworker at the Home Office[38]. If a reconsideration cannot be sought, then the avenue to challenge an adverse decision under MVDAC is by way of pre-action letter and judicial review (see Chapter 8).

---

36 UKVI Guidance, Settlement: customer service standards, 22 May 2023

37 See s.15 which amended s.82 of the Nationality, Immigration and Asylum Act 2002

38 Migrant Victims of Domestic Abuse Concession (formerly the destitute domestic violence concession (DDVC)) Version 4.0 04 April 2024 p11

CHAPTER THREE

MAKING A VALID APPLICATION FOR SETTLEMENT AS A VICTIM OF DOMESTIC ABUSE

We now turn to making an application for settlement under the immigration rules as victim of DV. Applications for ILR on this basis are now to be made under Appendix Victim of Domestic Abuse ('AVDA'). They were formerly made under Appendix FM DVILR[39].

As with all immigration applications, the starting point is to ensure that the application is a valid application. As per rule VDA 1.4, an application which does not meet validity requirements may be rejected as invalid and not considered.

Practitioners should be familiar with Paragraph 34 of the Immigration rules which sets out how to make a valid application for permission to stay in the UK.

---

https://webarchive.nationalarchives.gov.uk/ukgwa/20240130193858/https://www.gov.uk/guidance/immigration-rules/immigration-rules-appendix-fm-family-members

3.1 – Specified Forms

There are three specified forms that can be used under this route. The correct form must be completed dependent on the applicant's circumstances. The forms are as follows:

a. Where a victim is outside the UK owing to the TMA (which we address in Chapter 5 further) they must apply from outside the UK using the 'Return to the UK Form'[40] (see rule VDA 1.1). It is important to note that if children are applying for entry clearance with their parent on this basis they will need to complete their own entry clearance application (however they do need to complete the parts of the form which relate to DV or meet fee waiver requirements so long as this is all set out in the parent's application)[41];

b. Where the applicant is in the UK they must completed the SET (DV) form[42] and any child applying at the same time as their parent is to be included on this form (see rule VDA 1.2(a)));

c. Where a child of a victim of DA is applying at a different time to their parent they must use form SET (F)[43] (see rule VDA 1.2(b)).

All mandatory sections on the application form must be completed (Immigration Rule 34 (2)).

---

40 https://visas-immigration.service.gov.uk/apply-visa-type/funnel;

41 Home Office Policy Guidance Appendix Victim of Domestic Abuse Version 17.0 04 April 2024 p7

42 https://visas-immigration.service.gov.uk/product/set-dv

43 https://www.gov.uk/government/publications/application-to-settle-in-the-uk-as-a-child-under-18-form-setf/apply-online-form-setf

3.2 – Application Fees and Fee Waivers

The applicant must pay the application fee, unless they have been granted a fee waiver (rule VDA 1.3(c)). The application fee is at the time of writing this title £2,885.00[44].

An applicant will be exempt from paying an application fee if they are destitute. A person is considered to be destitute where they (a) do not have adequate accommodation or the means to obtain it (whether or not their essential living needs are met), or (b) they have adequate accommodation or the means of obtaining it but cannot meet their other essential living needs.

Detailed information on fee waivers is set out in the Home Office Policy Fee Waiver: Human Rights-based and other specified applications Version 6.0 08 April 2022, but this Guidance notes that the AVDA Policy provides separate and specific guidance on fee waivers for victims of DV.

Where an applicant says they are destitute they are to submit their application form and provide evidence that they have no means to pay the specified fee.

The assessment is based upon the individual's circumstances and those of their dependent family members, so it is very important an applicant explains this. However, the AVDA Policy Guidance is clear that where sufficient information and information is not provided additional enquiries can be made to see whether one qualifies[45]. The Policy also explains what sort of evidence and information might be expected, such as a tenancy agreement setting out cost of accommodation, evidence of income through bank statements or pay slips, evidence of outgoings such

---

44 Policy paper Home Office immigration and nationality fees: 10 April 2024

45 See p10-12

as utility bills, letter from a local authority or DWP, letters from a support organisation or friends regarding assistance with accommodation and finance[46], or a written letter from the applicant explaining their financial circumstances[47].

The AVDA Policy notes that there may be a reasonable explanation as to why documentary evidence may not be available. For example, when an individual is subject to financial abuse they may not hold or have access to a bank account, or be named on any documentation relating to income or outgoings[48].

In an TMA application an assessment of destitution will have regard to the persons circumstances in the UK if they return, including the costs of returning to the UK[49]. There is also an acknowledgment by the UKVI that it will be much harder for these applicants to provide evidence of their circumstances as they may be living with hostile family members or may be unable to inform those they live with of the fact they are making an application to return to the UK[50].

Where a fee waiver request is rejected the reasons for this must be set out in writing and the applicant must be told that to validate the application they must pay the specified fee within 10 working days. If the fee is not paid then the application will be rejected as invalid[51].

---

46 There is no expectation that a friend or family member supporting a victim should pay an application fee; p10.

47 See p10

48 See p11

49 Home Office Policy Guidance Appendix Victim of Domestic Abuse Version 17.0 04 April 2024 p9

50 Ibid. p11

51 Ibid. p12

3.3 – Biometrics

In accordance with VDA 1.3(d) the applicant must provide any required biometrics. This requirement can be dispensed with where the UKVI (a) excuse the individual from the requirement to enrol, or (b) make a decision to re-use previously enrolled biometrics.

The Home Office Guidance Unable to travel to a Visa Application Centre to enrol biometrics (overseas applications) (interim) Version 3.0 03 May 2024 is relevant to an application from abroad. This makes clear that it applies to individuals who are unable to travel to a Visa Application Centre ('VAC'). There are four criteria to excuse an individual from the requirement to attend a VAC. These include (i) satisfying the decision maker about their identity to a reasonable standard, (ii) providing evidence that they need to make an urgent journey to a VAC which is unsafe based on the current situation in the area they are located and the route they need to travel and they cannot delay their journey till later or use an alternate route, (iii) they must show their circumstances are so compelling as to make them exceptional, and (iv) they must explain why they cannot attend a VAC but are able to travel to the UK[52].

In regards to reusing biometrics for those in the UK, the Home Office Guidance Biometrics Reuse Version 5.0 dated 08 February 2024 states that the policy aim is to require foreign nationals to enrol their fingerprint biometric information only once so these can be used whenever the individual makes a new application. However, in most circumstances individuals must enrol a new facial image every time they make an immigration application as faces change unlike fingerprints[53].

---

[52] See pp12-26

[53] See p5

Applicants on the VDA route are not listed as individuals whose fingerprint biometrics can be reused[54]. As such, they will need to show that there are exceptional circumstances for reusing their biometrics where the UKVI retains the same. Exceptional circumstances include being physically unable to attend a biometric enrolment event or use the Immigration: ID check app, though the use of mobile enrolment or deferment of enrolment is to be considered first. It is said that circumstances where biometric reuse would be appropriate include where the person is incapacitated through disability or illness or injury or treatment, or where they lack mental capacity to cooperate with enrolment, or they are isolated to avoid contact with others to prevent harm or injury or illness[55].

3.4 – Passport/Document to Establish Identity and Nationality

The individual must also provide a passport or other document which satisfactorily establishes their identity and nationality; see rule VDA 1.3(e) and Paragraph 34(5)(a)(b) of the Immigration Rules.

In accordance with VDA 1.4 discretion can be exercised to treat an application as valid, if an individual is unable to provide proof of identity for one of the reasons set out under Paragraph 34(5)(c) of the rules[56].

---

[54] Home Office Guidance Biometrics Reuse Version 5.0 dated 08 February 2024, see p6

[55] Ibid. pp9-10

[56] 34(5)(c) Proof of identity need not be provided where: (i) the applicant's passport, national identity card or travel document is held by the Home Office at the date of application; or (ii) the applicant's passport, nationality identity card or travel document has been permanently lost or stolen and there is no functioning national government to issue a replacement; or (iii) the applicant's passport, nationality identity card or travel document has been retained by an employer or other person in circumstances which have led to the applicant being the subject of a positive conclusive grounds decision made by a competent authority

The reasons include showing a good reason beyond their control why they cannot provide proof of identity; see Paragraph 34(5)(c)(vii). It is of course not uncommon for an abuser to have possession of a victim of DA's passport and documents and this may be considered as a good reason why a victim cannot produce the same.

As per rule 34(5)(6), the Secretary of State may ask an applicant to provide alternative satisfactory evidence of their identity and nationality. The AVDA Policy Guidance sets out alternative documents that can be accepted[57], though the list is non-exhaustive. These include for example national identity cards, BRPs, birth certificates or other source documents issued by national authorities, ID documents issued by non-governmental organisations, expired passports or other travel documents. This Guidance makes clear that the decision whether to accept alternate documents will depend on several factors such as where the application is being made from, the process applied by an authority when it issues an ID document, whether the person enrols their biometrics, whether their circumstances are so compelling that the documentation should be accepted.

The AVDA Policy notes that individuals seeking settlement will have been granted leave previously as a partner and Home Office records can be consulted to make a decision on an application[58].

---

under the National Referral Mechanism; or (iv) the application is for limited leave to enable access to public funds pending an application under paragraph 289A of, or under Part 6 of Appendix Armed Forces; or (v) the application is made under Part 14 of these rules, for leave as the family member of a stateless person; or (vi) the application was made by a person in the UK with refugee leave or humanitarian protection; or (vii) the applicant provides a good reason beyond their control why they cannot provide proof of their identity.

57 See p8

58 See p8

Victims can approach the police where a passport or documents have been taken by an abuser, but it is common that there is real reluctance to approach the authorities. Applicants may find it easier to apply for a new passport instead of asking for discretion to be exercised given the above process.

CHAPTER FOUR

MEETING THE SUITABILITY AND ELIGIBILITY REQUIREMENTS UNDER THE IMMIGRATION RULES AS A MIGRANT VICTIM OF DOMESTIC ABUSE

We now move on to look at the suitability and eligibility requirements for individuals seeking settlement under Appendix Victim of Domestic Abuse.

4.1 – Suitability

At VDA 2.1 it is made clear that an applicant must not fall for refusal under the Immigration Rules, Part 9 of the General Grounds for Refusal. As such it is important that practitioners are familiar with Part 9 of the Immigration Rules.

An exception to this is that the Rules make clear that Paragraph 9.8.4 of the Rules does not apply to this route. Paragraph 9.8.4 deals with the scenario of an individual who falls for refusal on the grounds that they have breached immigration laws by overstaying their permission to stay. Overstay will not be a ground of refusal for applications under AVDA. The AVDA Policy makes clear that this is in recognition of the fact that victims may not be able to apply whilst they hold leave. This is because their documents, e.g., passports may be taken from them, the individual may as such not be aware of when their leave expires or may be told by their abusive partners dishonestly that their status is being dealt with when it in fact is not.

A separate book can be written on Part 9 of the General Grounds of Refusal within the Immigration Rules. As such, in this chapter I will simply highlight some factors and materials that practitioners should be familiar with when dealing with issues that arise in respect of suitability.

Within Part 9 of the Immigration Rules there are mandatory grounds of refusal and discretionary grounds of refusal.

Mandatory grounds of refusal include for example, where an individual is subject to a deportation or exclusion order[59], where they have been convicted of a criminal offence for which they have received a custodial sentence of 12 months or more[60], where the decision can prove that it is more likely than not that the applicant used deception in an application[61]. Please note mandatory grounds of refusal are far more extensive than this.

Discretionary grounds of refusal include where in relation to an application for permission to stay in order to obtain documents from the Home Office or a third party in support of the application false representations are made or false information or documents are submitted or relevant facts are not disclosed[62], where an individual fails without reasonable excuse to comply with a reasonable requirement to attend an interview or provide information[63], or where a relevant NHS body has notified the Home Office that an individual has failed to pay charges under the NHS regulation on charges to overseas visitors and the outstanding charges have a total value of at least £500[64].

---

59 Paragraph 9.2.1(c)

60 Paragraph 9.4.1(a)

61 Paragraph 9.7.2

62 Paragraph 9.7.1(a)(b)

63 Paragraph 9.9.1(a)(b)

64 Paragraph 9.11.1

There is a range of policy guidance publications issued on General Grounds of Refusal[65], in particular I highlight the Suitability: non-conducive grounds for refusal or cancellation of entry clearance or permission[66], Suitability: false representations, deception, false documents, non-disclosure of relevant facts[67], Grounds for Refusal – Criminality[68] and Suitability: Exclusion and Deportation[69].

In respect of discretionary grounds of refusal, it is important advisors are aware that parts of the guidance[70] and authorities[71] refer to the need for a balancing exercise of negative factors weighing against the individual against positive factors weighing in their favour. It is as such important that arguments and information are advanced at an early stage.

Advisors should also take careful instructions on why any suitability issues arise. For example, an individual may have a conviction for fare evasion, theft, assault but this may have arisen owing to them being a victim of domestic violence. They may have been subject to financial control or have acted in self-defence. An NHS debt may have arisen owing to injuries sustained in domestic abuse. A victim may still be living in a matrimonial home or with family and may not have access to emails or post, they may as such have been unaware of any requirement to attend

65 https://www.gov.uk/government/collections/general-grounds-for-refusal-modernised-guidance

66 Version 3.0 dated 16 January 2024

67 Version 4.0 dated 14 November 2023

68 Version 3.0 dated 16 January 2024

69 Version 2.0 dated 16 January 2024

70 See for example the Suitability: false representations, deception, false documents, non-disclosure of relevant facts at p21 and for example Grounds for Refusal – Criminality at p5, p16, p19

71 See for example *Ngouh, R (on the application of) v Secretary of State for the Home Department* [2010] EWHC 2218 (Admin) at para.120

an interview or provide further information or documents. The AVDA Policy states that on discretionary grounds 'the impact of wider domestic abuse may give rise to not apply the ground' and 'criminal convictions that relate to the domestic abuse must not be considered in an assessment of whether the applicant's presence is not conducive to the public good'[72].

The AVDA Policy also makes clear that even where an application falls for refusal on suitability requirements, decision makers must go on to consider and set out whether an individual meets the eligibility requirements[73]. We as such will now move on to consider eligibility requirements.

4.2 – Eligibility

I address eligibility requirements for victims of transnational marriage abandonment, who are making entry clearance applications, in Chapter 5 at length. I will not repeat this here but I do highlight that there are different requirements in these cases to be complied with. In this section I focus upon requirements for victims of domestic violence that are seeking settlement under AVDA whilst they are in the UK.

4.2.1 – Relationship Requirement

Victims must have held leave as a partner in the right category. The best way to explain who is eligible is to read the rules directly. I as such set these out here. Under VDA 4.1(a-f) an individual must have or have last been given permission to stay in one of the following categories:

72 See p13

73 See p13

- a partner under Appendix FM (except for permission as a fiancé(e) or proposed civil partner) of a person who is a British citizen, settled in the UK or an EEA national in the UK with limited leave to enter or remain granted under paragraph EU3 of Appendix EU on the basis of meeting condition 1 in paragraph EU14 of Appendix EU; or

- a spouse, civil partner or durable partner under Appendix EU with limited leave to enter or remain as a family member of a relevant EEA citizen (or of a qualifying British citizen), as a joining family member of a relevant sponsor or as a family member who has retained the right of residence, granted under paragraph EU3 or EU3A of that Appendix; or

- a partner under Appendix FM, Part 11, or Appendix Family Reunion (Protection) of a person with permission as a refugee; or

- a partner of a person present and settled in the UK under paragraph 285 or 295E of Part 8; or

- a victim of domestic abuse under Appendix FM; or

- a partner under Appendix Armed Forces or Part 7 (except for permission as a fiancé(e) or proposed civil partner), of any of the below:

    - person who is a British citizen; or

    - a foreign and commonwealth citizen with at least 4 years' reckonable service in HM Forces at the date of application under this paragraph; or

    - a member of HM Armed forces who has applied for or been granted permission or settlement as a foreign and commonwealth citizen discharged from HM Armed Forces; Or

- leave outside the rules granted under the Migrant Victims of Domestic Abuse Concession (formerly the destitution domestic violence concession (DDVC)), and before that were last granted permission under one of the categories defined in VDA 4.1(a) to (e).

Most of these categories are self-explanatory. However, I will expand upon some of these.

Under VDA 4.1(a) partners under Appendix FM include both those granted leave under the 5 year partner route and those granted leave under the 10-year partner route.

The class of individuals referred to at VDA 4.1(aa) is a recent expansion to this route (as of 4 April 2024). This allows a spouse, civil partner or unmarried partner with pre-settled status as a partner under the EU Settlement Scheme ('EUSS') to apply for settlement as a victim of DA.

Prior to this amendment to the immigration rules[74] partners with pre-settled status under EUSS could apply for status independent of their partner under Appendix EU where they were subjected to domestic violence, but if they were unable to demonstrate 5 years continuous residence they would only qualify for pre-settled status. It is not hard to see how this was considered to be unfair, with partners of British nationals, refugees and partners of EU nationals granted leave under Appendix FM being entitled to access the MVDA concession and settlement where subjected to DV regardless of their length of time in the UK, but partners of EU nationals only being treated differently and

[74] Statement of Changes in Immigration Rules HC 590

having no access to the MVDA concession and to potentially having to wait many years for settlement.

This discrimination was challenged in the High Court in 2023. The proceedings were settled by consent with the Home Office agreeing to review their policies and using reasonable endeavours to publish the outcome of that review by 16 May 2024. The Statement of Reasons which accompanied the consent order stating as follows:

> "4. The Defendant now admits that he breached the Claimant's rights under Article 14 ECHR, read with Article 8 by treating her (as a victim of domestic violence with pre-settled status under Appendix EU) less favourably than a victim of domestic violence with limited leave to remain under Appendix FM. The Defendant accepts that the Claimant's treatment fell within the ambit of Article 8, that she had a relevant status as a person with Appendix EU leave who had suffered domestic violence, that she was in an analogous situation to persons with Appendix FM leave who had suffered domestic violence and that there was no justification for treating the Claimant differently.
>
> 5. The Defendant has agreed to review the DDV concession policy and use his reasonable endeavours to publish the outcome of the review by 16 May 2024. The Defendant accepts that the review of the policy is long overdue (including because its current published terms are inaccurate, something which the Court of Appeal has noted is *"highly regrettable to say the least"* (per Singh LJ in *R (SWP) v SSHD* [2023] 4 WLR 37). Unless the Defendant uses reasonable endeavours to publish the outcome of his review

> by 16 May 2024, the Claimant has liberty to restore proceedings."[75]

The Home Office explained when introducing the changes to this rule that this was being done to 'ensure that partners of EEA and Swiss citizens with EUSS status are treated equally under these domestic abuse provisions, regardless of whether the relationship was formed before or after the end of the transition period[76].'

I am not a welfare benefits lawyer but as I refer to earlier on in this book, those who hold pre-settled status can face difficulties in accessing public funds too owing to the need to meet the right to reside test[77]. The ability to seek leave through MVDAC and ILR though AVDA can assist with these complications, though advice from a welfare benefits lawyer should also be taken.

There may however be advantages to staying with leave under the EUSS scheme. I set out some matters to consider below, though the differences between EUSS status and this route are vaster than I have put here. This however provides some food for thought:

- An applicant may, for example, be very close to qualifying for settlement under Appendix EU. It may be worth considering how long they have to wait to reach 5 years.

- Those with leave under EUSS have enhanced rights. For example, settled status is only lost after a period of 5 years absence

---

75 https://www.centralenglandlc.org.uk/Handlers/Download.ashx?IDMF=7fad50e1-55de-4288-b8ea-74960ead8ad5

76 Explanatory Memorandum to The Statement of Changes in Immigration Rules presented to Parliament on 14 March 2023 (HC 590) at paragraph 5.24

77 See *Secretary of State for Work and Pensions v AT* [2024] 2 W.L.R. 967

from the UK[78] whereas ILR is lost after a period of 2 years' absence from the UK[79].

- Moreover, whilst the breakdown of a relationship leads to a loss of status for a spouse of say a British national, the same does not apply for spouses of EU nationals under Appendix EU. Spouses of EU nationals can apply for pre-settled status on the basis of retained rights (following for e.g., termination of the marriage), not just on the basis of domestic violence.

- It is also important to note that whilst a victim may qualify for leave under the MVDA concession, they would then have to qualify for ILR under AVDA. If the AVDA application was refused, for example owing to the fact the Home Office did not accept that the relationship broke down owing to DV, they would not have a right of appeal against a refusal (though they would have one against a refusal under Appendix EU). They would instead have a right to administrative review and if the negative decision was upheld at administrative review stage then they would thereafter be without leave whilst pursuing any judicial review or further application. They would have lost their rights under EUSS by being granted leave under the MVDAC and so would have to then make a new application under Appendix EU.

It can be seen from the above why thorough and carefully considered advice, on a case-by-case basis, is required for these cases.

See for example https://commission.europa.eu/system/files/2022-10/q-a-uk-citizens-declaratory-countries_en_0.pdf – paras. 2.16, 4.5 and 7.4

79 See for example, Home Office Policy Guidance Lapsing Leave and Returning Residents Version 8.0 dated 16 January 2024 at p4

VDA 4.1(b) allows for the partner of a refugee to qualify for settlement[80]. This was an amendment which was made to the previous rules (Appendix FM E-DVILR 1.2), following litigation. In the case of *A v SSHD* [2016] ScotCS CSIH 38 it was found that the domestic violence provisions discriminated against spouses of refugees in that they were previously not included in the provisions as one of the categories permitted to make an application under these rules. It was said that statistical material before the court indicated that some 95% of refugees granted 5-year leave were later granted ILR at the end of that period and the grounds upon which refugee status were lost or an individual expelled were very limited[81]. It was considered that given the underlying aim of the domestic violence provisions, the expectations of partners of refugees in respect of gaining settlement, that for spouses of refugees the difference in treatment was not justified or proportionate[82].

Readers may be wondering why VDA 4.1(d) refers to individuals with leave under the previous version of these rules, Appendix FM DV-ILR. This addresses the former version of the rules which contained D-DVILR 1.2, which said that where an individual did not qualify for leave owing to the fact they did not meet suitability grounds S-ILR 1.5[83] or S-ILR 1.6[84], the individual would be granted leave for no more than 30 months.

---

80 Please note this does not include partners of individuals who hold humanitarian protection.

81 See Paras. 67-68 of *A v SSHD* [2016] ScotCS CSIH 38

82 Ibid. Paras. 66, 79-82

83 S-ILR.1.5. The presence of the applicant in the UK is not conducive to the public good because they have been convicted of an offence for which they have been sentenced to imprisonment for less than 12 months, unless a period of 7 years has passed since the end of the sentence.

84 S-ILR.1.6. The applicant has, within the 24 months preceding the date of the application, been convicted of or admitted an offence for which they received a non-custodial sentence or other out of court disposal that is recorded on their criminal record.

These individuals will of course need to seek further leave and so VDA 4.1(d) allows for them to apply for settlement.

VDA 4.1(f) prevents the partners of workers and students that qualify for the MVDAC concession from applying for ILR.

Please note that whilst an individual has to have held leave in the correct category, that leave does not need to be extant at the time of the application. This is in recognition of the fact they may be an overstayer as a result of the abuse they have faced (see section 4.1 of this Chapter on Suitability)[85].

For those that meet the relationship requirement, they will then have to satisfy VDA 4.2 which we will move on to consider shortly.

Where an individual does not meet the relationship requirement, then all may not be lost and there may still be scope for argument depending on the circumstances. See Chapter 7 of this book[86].

4.2.2 – Domestic Violence Cause of Relationship Breakdown

VDA 4.2 requires that '[t]he relationship between the applicant and their partner must have broken down permanently as a result of domestic abuse.'

Timing or Date of Violence

Some relationships start out well and violence occurs at a later stage. It is also not uncommon for victims to endure months or even years of

[85] See also Home Office Policy Guidance Appendix Victim of Domestic Abuse Version 17.0 04 April 2024 p18

[86] Ibid. pp18-19

violence. It is however important to note that the fact that a relationship may breakdown owing to violence at a very early stage in a relationship this is not to be treated as an adverse factor[87].

Practitioners may note that this version of the rule has been amended (significantly) from the previous version in E-DVILR 1.3 which read as follows,

> "*The applicant must provide evidence that during the last period of limited leave* as a partner of a British Citizen, a person present and settled in the UK, a person with refugee leave, or a person in the UK with limited leave under Appendix EU in accordance with paragraph GEN.1.3.(d), under paragraph D-ECP.1.1., DLTRP.1.1 or D-LTRP.1.2 of this Appendix, *or during their only period of permission under Appendix Family Reunion (Protection), the applicant's relationship with their partner broke down permanently as a result of domestic abuse*" (emphasis added)

As can be seen from the underlined wording above, the previous version of the rules required that the relationship broke down owing to domestic violence during the last period of leave as a partner[88]. Consider an Applicant who was granted leave as a partner for 2.5 years. She is subjected to controlling behaviour throughout the marriage and her partner tells her he is dealing with her visa application. He does not do so and she becomes an overstayer. Whilst an overstayer she is subjected to physical violence and hospitalised. As the abuse occurred after her last period of leave under the rules, she would not have qualified for settlement owing to E-DVILR 1.3. However, the amended version of this provision in VDA 4.2 would allow this applicant to qualify. This is

87 Ibid. p22

88 See *IN (Domestic violence – IDI – policy) Pakistan* [2000] UKAIT 00024

a welcome change to these rules which is likely to assist numerous victims.

Appendix VDA 4.2 is however the requirement that most applications are likely to be refused under, given E-DVILR 1.3 was the provision that lawyers saw the most refusals under previously.

Cause of Breakdown

It can be seen from the wording of the provision that what an applicant needs to show is that the relationship broke down permanently *as a result of* domestic violence. It is not uncommon for relationships to deteriorate over time and for there to be many reasons why this occurs. The Home Office may argue that the relationship has not broken down permanently owing to domestic violence and that there is another cause of the relationship having broken down.

Where the factual history of a marriage breakdown is complicated the case of *LA (para 289A: causes of breakdown) Pakistan* [2009] UKAIT 00019 is useful to refer to. The Tribunal held at paragraph 36 that a decision maker "must be careful to assess the evidence in the round, looking at the totality of the evidence and remembering that a broken marriage may have ended before the parties separate and the marriage may have broken down as a result of domestic violence even if other grounds are given in matrimonial proceedings or raised before the Tribunal." It may be, as was said in *AG (India) v Secretary of State for the Home Department* [2007] EWCA Civ 1534 at para. 19 that whilst there were several problems in a marriage ultimately "the husband was a violent and cruel man, and those characteristics of his could not be separated out from the end of the marriage.

Advisors should take instructions and prepare evidence with care where these issues arise.

Burden and Standard of Proof

The burden of proof is on the applicant to show that they meet the rules.

The standard of proof in these claims (aside from in transnational marriage abandonment cases which I discuss in Chapter 5), is the balance of probabilities[89]. This means an applicant has to demonstrate that it is more likely than not that they meet the requirements of the immigration rules. This means that there is at least a 51% likelihood of the applicant's account being true.

Evidence of Violence

It can of course be very difficult to evidence domestic violence and this has long been recognised; see *Ishtiaq v Secretary of State for the Home Department* [2007] EWCA Civ 386 for example[90].

Violence often occurs indoors in one's home and emotional abuse, or controlling behaviour for example can be difficult for a victim to recognise as violence or seen by others. Discussing or disclosing domestic violence can also be extremely challenging.

The AVDA Policy sets out a list of evidence that might be produced in a claim and explains what weight the Home Office should attach to different types of evidence.

---

89 Home Office Policy Guidance Appendix Victim of Domestic Abuse Version 17.0 04 April 2024 pp21

90 para 17; See also Home Office Policy Guidance Appendix Victim of Domestic Abuse Version 17.0 04 April 2024 pp21-22

It is important to note that it is said 'the list of evidence is not exhaustive, and applicants can rely on any relevant evidence to support their application.[91]

With the above in mind, I turn to consider the list of evidence in the AVDA Policy. Please note that whilst I summarise parts of the Guidance here[92], there is of course no replacement for reading this document in full.

Some evidence is described in the AVDA Policy as conclusive evidence, this means that it 'is sufficient to meet the requirements of VDA 4.2. No further consideration of other evidence is required.' This evidence includes for example:

- a criminal conviction or police caution which relates to DV,
- a final order in a civil court where a judge has found domestic violence has occurred or where admissions have been made by the abuser (e.g., non-molestation order or occupation order),
- a charging decision from the Crown Prosecution Service,
- a Multi-agency risk assessment conference referral confirmed by a person who is a member of MARAC,
- a prohibited steps orders / contact orders / specific issue orders / disclosure of whereabouts orders / port alert order / securing a child's passport order / order to recover a child / as well as High Court orders using the court's inherent jurisdiction where there

[91] Ibid. p31

[92] Home Office Policy Guidance Appendix Victim of Domestic Abuse Version 17.0 04 April 2024 pp32-41

has been fact finding and there is evidence that domestic abuse was a factor in granting the order.

Other evidence is described as 'compelling' or 'can be compelling' in the AVDA Policy, dependent on the circumstances and information contained in the evidence and any surrounding evidence. This includes for example:

- A final order in a civil court (e.g., non-molestation order or occupation order) where there is finding of fact recorded,
- A Domestic Violence Protection Order made by the magistrates court on the application of the police,
- Domestic Abuse Protection Notices and Domestic Abuse Protection Orders,
- Female Genital Mutilation Protection Orders,
- Forced Marriage Protection Orders,
- Contemporaneous emails, texts, social media conversations or photos could be compelling evidence if they outline incidences of abuse or back up other evidence provided,
- Correspondence with one or more of the abusive parties that reveals threatening or abusive behaviour may also be compelling if the source of the communications can be verified,
- A letter from social services, or a welfare officer connected to HM Armed Forces confirming that the writer of the letter has themselves assessed the individual and has sufficient experience to consider them as a victim of DA,

- A Letter from an organisation supporting victims of domestic abuse (including a refuge) confirming that they have assessed the applicant as being a victim of domestic abuse, what support is being provided and if no support why not. The Guidance states that the letter should not merely be relaying the applicant's account,

- A medical report from a UK hospital or from GP or from a medical professional, employed by HM Armed Forces confirming injuries or a condition consistent with domestic abuse, dependent on the contents of the report. It is again said that less weight will be given where the notes reflect the account reported by the individual.

Given medical evidence is often seen in these claims, we will delve into this further. Often what is said is that letters from a GP surgery or other medical professional are simply repeating or recording what the applicant has stated. This is more often than not unlikely to be the case as where injuries are recorded in notes they will have most likely been inspected by a doctor. Where medication is prescribed or treatment is recommended (e.g., physiotherapy or counselling) this will be based on an examination and/or diagnosis and the doctor exercising their critical faculties and clinical experience. Referrals to a DV support organisations are often made by GPs and this is following an assessment that this is what the individual requires and is the doctor's independent opinion. There is a useful analysis of medical evidence in DV claims in *R (on the application of) Balakaoohi v SSHD* [2012] EWHC 1439[93].

The AVDA Guidance says that the weight to be attached to police attendance at a domestic abuse incident is dependent on the contents of any evidence. In contrast, an arrest is not considered in the Guidance to be convincing evidence as it is said an arrest is based upon suspicion. Where there is an arrest it is said further information may be sought from

[93] See paragraphs 91-92

the police. *Balakaoohi* [2012] EWHC 1439 is again a useful decision where such evidence exists, as it demonstrates at paras. 86-87 the need for detailed analysis of police records.

The weight attached to a letter or statement from independent witness will depend on whether they have witnessed an incident of DA and the relationship they have with the victim, i.e., they gain nothing from supporting the case, they are not too closely connected to the victim. Please note that the Courts have taken a different approach to the Home Office on this sort of evidence. Indeed what has been said is that 'witness statements from friends or family members and letters from official sources that relay unfounded reports by the applicant should be verified where possible and treated as additional evidence when building up the case background.'[94]

Similarly, a statement from an applicant will depend on the detail and the information contained within the same. Applying the guidance set out in *Balakaoohi* [2012] EWHC 1439 at §35(8) and (9), the AVDA Policy states 'Where limited evidence is available, in particular where the only evidence available is a statement from the applicant, consideration should be given to any reasons provided for the lack of documentary evidence in support of the application, in particular where any reasons arise from or otherwise relate to the abusive relationship or situation the applicant is or was in'[95]. Please note that *Balakaoohi* [2012] EWHC 1439 also held at §35(11) 'a caseworker can rarely decide whether a report by the applicant is unfounded without interviewing the applicant and asking questions about the alleged domestic violence.' It may as such be worth inviting the Home Office to interview an applicant in an appropriate case where evidence is lacking and to explain at length in statements and covering letters why evidence is indeed unavailable.

94 *Balakaoohi* [2012] EWHC 1439 at para 35(7)

95 Home Office Policy Guidance Appendix Victim of Domestic Abuse Version 17.0 04 April 2024 p31

As can be seen from the above, a lot will depend on the content of and detail in the evidence when considered under the Guidance. Reading this may concern a lot of practitioners given how hard it can be to obtain documents in these cases. As such, I highlight a few matters that may assist practitioners with submissions and challenges:

- The Guidance makes clear that all evidence should be considered in the round[96] or holistically, which means the Home Office should be reading and assessing the documents together rather than looking at each piece of evidence in isolation[97].

- 'If it had been intended that applicants could only prove that they have been the victims of domestic violence by producing documents of the kind specified in the [guidance], this could have been achieved easily enough in the rule. One way of doing it would have been to specify the necessary documents in the rule itself.'[98]

- As has been said by the Court of Appeal the Home Office Guidance 'is not inflexibly prescriptive'[99] and it is not the purpose of the rules to deny ILR to victims of DV 'who can prove their case but cannot do so in one of the ways that have been prescribed by the Secretary of State in his instructions to caseworkers.'[100]

---

96 Ibid.

97 See *Balakaoohi* [2012] EWHC 1439 at paras. 103 and 107 as an example in this regard

98 Ibid. at para 32

99 *Ishtiaq* [2007] EWCA Civ 386 at para. 41

100 Ibid. at para. 31

- '[T]he caseworker in reaching a decision should use the IDIs as guidance and not as a mandatory series of prescriptive steps which must lead to an unfavourable decision for the applicant if any step provided for in the guidance cannot be fulfilled.' [101]

- '[L]ack of police involvement or criminal prosecution or a conviction is not an adverse factor in itself.'[102]

- Some applicants may state they have had difficulties disclosing domestic violence to authorities owing to the presence of family members or interpreter issues[103]. Individuals may not be registered with a GP, they may be worried about contacting the authorities owing to a lack of advice and understanding and fears about their status, they may be isolated. Like the applicant in *R (Suliman) v Secretary of State for the Home Department* [2020] EWHC 326 (Admin), the victim may be embarrassed, ashamed, still love their partner, want the relationship to work, be scared of losing their partner, not want their partner to get into any trouble[104]. Where explanations like these are given then the Home Office must engage with this and address the same[105].

---

101 *Balakaoohi* [2012] EWHC 1439 at para 35(12)

102 Home Office Policy Guidance Appendix Victim of Domestic Abuse Version 17.0 04 April 2024 p22

103 *AN (Pakistan) v SSHD* [2010] EWCA Civ 757 at paras. 31 and 51 for example

104 At para. 25

105 Ibid.

- The UKVI acknowledge that trauma as a result of DV may impact ability to recount events chronologically and could result in inconsistencies in an account[106].

In addition to the above, the AVDA Policy requires caseworkers to deal with cases sensitively, flexibly, and cooperatively allowing applicants to be given a chance to show they are eligible for ILR. The Guidance in fact sets out a detailed process by which applicants, who do not fall for refusal on suitability grounds, must be contacted for further information or evidence. Please note that the guidance mandates that contact be made twice, that requests should be clear in what is being sought, contact must be made safely with individuals not being contacted at the abuser's address, allowing for sufficient time for a response, agreeing to reasonable extension of time requests. Caseworkers must exercise discretion in an applicant's favour during this process, reducing administrative burdens[107].

Where necessary or where an applicant states that records in support of their claim might be available from the police, the passport office or another authority, consideration should be given by the UKVI, on a case-by-case basis, to making enquiries on behalf of an applicant in line with GDPR and other data protection measures[108]. This can be useful given there can be real delays in obtaining disclosure from the police. This may be particularly necessary where there are pending prosecutions against an abuser or there has been a police caution issued against a perpetrator[109]. This is in recognition of the fact that an individual may not be able to produce evidence in such a claim, though in order to assist the Home Office in making checks in these cases as much information as is available

---

[106] Home Office Policy Guidance Appendix Victim of Domestic Abuse Version 17.0 04 April 2024 p21

[107] Ibid. p43

[108] Ibid. pp31 and 43

[109] Ibid. Pp44-45

should be provided including names, addresses, nationality, and date of birth.

I also highlight that the SET (DV) application form seeks evidence of the applicant having lived with their partner prior to the breakdown. This is undoubtedly to show that the relationship was subsisting. It is important to note this is not a mandatory requirement under the immigration rules and indeed it may be difficult to obtain such evidence, particularly in a controlling relationship. However, where it can be obtained such evidence might include utility bills, council tax, bank statements, letters from the NHS, letters from a landlord or a tenancy agreement.

Counter Claims

It is not uncommon to get counter claims from an abusive partner sent to the Home Office directly, or for letters to be sent from a partner to inform the UKVI that the relationship has broken down for other reasons, or indeed for a perpetrator of violence to become aware of an application to UKVI on the grounds of DV and to write in to state that they deny any allegations made against them or to give a different version of events.

The AVDA Policy says caseworkers 'can sometimes consider counterclaims and denials as evidence alongside an application', balancing the evidence presented by both sides and deciding whether the applicant's account is credible on the balance of probabilities (or on the lower standard for transnational marriage abandonment cases)[110].

It is also said if there is 'third party corroborative' evidence supporting a victim's account any denial or counter claim made can be disregarded, though there is also allowance in the Policy for the UKVI to make their

110 Ibid. p48

own enquiries (i.e., with the police if there is a suggestion they were involved)[111].

Applicants may have concerns about this process and in fact they may be completely unaware of what has been sent to the Home Office by an abusive partner. There may be good arguments to advance about the fairness of this process. As was said in *R v Secretary of State for the Home Department, ex p. Doody* [1994] 1 A.C. 531 at 560 'The principles of fairness are not to be applied by rote identically in every situation. What fairness demands is dependent on the context of the decision, and this is to be taken into account in all its aspects... Fairness will very often require that a person who may be adversely affected by the decision will have an opportunity to make representations on his own behalf either before the decision is taken with a view to producing a favourable result; or after it is taken, with a view to procuring its modification; or both... Since the person affected usually cannot make worthwhile representations without knowing what factors may weigh against his interests fairness will very often require that he is informed of the gist of the case which he has to answer.'[112]

Children

As discussed in Chapter 6 dependent children can also apply with their parent or after their parent has applied; see VDA 5.1-8.2.

---

111 Ibid.

112 See also *Balajigari v The Secretary of State for the Home Department* [2019] EWCA Civ 673 at paras. 45-61

Decisions

Where a victim of DA meets all the above requirements their entry clearance application for settlement will be granted; see VDA 9.1 and 10.2.

If an application is refused, the applicant can challenge an adverse decision by administrative review; see VDA 9.2 and Chapter 8 of this title.

CHAPTER FIVE

DEALING WITH TRANSNATIONAL MARRIAGE ABANDONMENT DOMESTIC VIOLENCE CASES

Transnational marriage abandonment (TMA) is an occurrence where foreign spouses or partners are purposely stranded abroad, in their home countries, by their UK national, settled or resident partners and/or their partner's families who then return to the UK without them. TMA has been recognised as domestic violence for some time[113] and tends to be a part of other abuse and control against a migrant victim.

Stranded spouses face several problems. These include often being separated from their British children in the UK, or being abandoned with their children abroad, being left without any financial support so they have no means to return, being unable to assert their rights in family law proceedings (in respect of their children, any property or assets, maintenance, dowry), being ostracized by their own families and society owing to the stigma associated with marriage breakdown/divorce, being at risk of violence from their own families or in laws in their home country. Their documents, including their visas and passports, are often kept by the abusive partners so that they are unable to travel back to the UK. Their visas may have expired or be close to expiry, which may also prevent their return to the UK. Abusers may contact the UKVI and inform them that the relationship has broken down in the hope this will result in the victim's visa being cancelled. The abusive partner may have

113 Family Procedure Rules – Practice Direction 12J – Child Arrangements & Contact Orders: Domestic Abuse And Harm, 2B

initiated divorce proceedings in the applicant's home country without their knowledge or consent.

5.1 – The History of TMA

Stranded spouses were also discriminated against, as the previous version of the immigration rules on domestic violence, namely Appendix FM DV-ILR, were drafted in a way that meant that they were unable to apply for settlement as victims of domestic violence because they were outside of the UK. Thankfully this has been rectified with Appendix VDA.

Before we go on to look at Appendix VDA, practitioners may be interested to learn about the way in which the lack of provision for TMA in the previous rules impacted upon victims of DV and their children, and how Appendix VDA came into force.

S (A Child), Re (Guidance in cases of stranded spouses) [2011] 1 FLR 305 gave important guidance on when an abandoned spouse was separated from minor children in the UK, prior to Appendix VDA coming into force. The case involved a Pakistani national female ('F'). She had an arranged marriage on 14 February 2008 to her British husband (of Pakistani origin). She was granted a spouse visa of just over two years in October 2008. When in the UK she said she was subjected to domestic abuse. In early 2010 F's husband and father-in-law took her to Pakistan and left her at her family home. She was bought a one-way ticket, whilst the others were purchased a return ticket. F did not want to go as she wanted to stay with their newborn son in the UK. F's son was left with his paternal grandmother in the UK whilst the mother was taken to Pakistan. She said she was given pills before the journey. Her husband said he divorced her in Pakistan. Her passport and Pakistani ID were taken from her when the husband and his father returned to the UK. F made an application from Pakistan in respect of her son. The Court found that she was deliberately stranded and separated from her child. They noted that despite the fact that the High Commission and Home Office were aware of her difficulties and the proceedings, she had not been granted a duplicate spouse visa to enable her to travel to the UK (though following the judgment she was given a six-month visa to participate in welfare proceedings for the child). Helpfully, Hogg J gave extensive guidance in stranded spouse cases. It included making a Tipstaff Passport Order to search for and seize the spouse's passport where it is alleged it has been taken, making a request for disclosure from the Home Office in form EX660 at the ex-parte stage to ascertain the spouse's immigration status to enable arrangements to be made for transfer of an existing visa and to obtain immigration advice, having an urgent fact finding hearing to investigate and ascertain the circumstances in which the parent and child came to be stranded internationally, if the stranded spouse's presence in the jurisdiction was necessary for the determination of the child's welfare to include directions in orders which may assist with a parent's application to enter the jurisdiction, considering ordering or inviting the abusing family members to fund flights for the stranded spouse and making an order for costs at the end of proceedings where they refuse to do so. Practitioners may be interested in reading and considering the guidance in full.

Despite the Home Office being made aware of cases like *S (A Child)*, there was no change in immigration rules to assist abandoned partners like F. This was thankfully challenged in *AM, R (On the Application Of) v SSHD* [2023] 1 WLR 732.

AM was a national of Pakistan. She married IM, a British national. In December 2017 she arrived in the UK on a spouse visa valid until August 2020. In December 2018 AM gave birth to a daughter. AM was subjected to physical, financial, emotional and sexual domestic violence in her marriage. This resulted in serious long-lasting injuries and hospitalisation. The Family Division of the High Court made very serious findings of abuse against IM. In December 2020, IM forced AM to travel to Pakistan in what he said was a holiday to resolve their marital problems. She refused to go initially and disclosed fears to social services that she would be abandoned there. Owing to threats made to her family in Pakistan, she agreed to go. The family travelled to Pakistan in January

2021. IM stayed with his family. AM and her daughter stayed with her family. In mid-January 2021, IM collected the daughter and did not return her.

AM contacted the British Embassy in Pakistan in March 2021 who suggested she apply for a replacement BRP. Unfortunately, the application was refused as she did not have valid leave when she left the UK. AM then instructed legal representatives who applied for a fee waiver explaining the history for AM and that she needed to be in the UK by 1 July 2021 to attend family proceedings. AM had to lodge a judicial review in respect of delay which resulted in the Upper Tribunal making an order that the UKVI make a decision on the fee waiver within a week. This resulted in the fee waiver being granted. Her solicitors then made an application for Indefinite Leave to Enter on the grounds of domestic violence. AM was granted 6 months LOTR with no recourse to public funds. AM entered the UK on 20 August 2021. The Family Court made an interim order that the child be returned to AM's care but owing to the NRPF condition this did not occur until 26 September 2021 when she was provided with accommodation.

AM challenged the decision to only grant her limited leave for 6 months with an NRPF condition. On 9 November 2021 she was granted 30 months leave. On 24 June 2022 she was granted ILR. Owing to the grant of ILR the Defendant argued that the claim was academic but Lieven J found that it was not. She held that 'it is very hard for the abandoned spouses to get the correct legal advice, to access funds to do so, and that there may be very considerable delay before they can do so. There is therefore considerable risk of injustice and hardship both to the women concerned, and their children, if this issue is not determined. There may also be a cohort of women who never do get the correct advice and are therefore hidden from any statistics as to the breadth of the problem… if this occasion before the Court is not taken there will be further delay and potentially injustice before the issue is determined.'[114]

AM's legal team argued that the DV-ILR rules were unlawful as they failed to make provision for stranded spouses and this failed to meet the purpose of the rules, to allow abused women to remain in the UK when their relationship had broken down owing to domestic violence. The Secretary of State argued that the cases could be addressed by applicants raising exceptional circumstances and by a grant of LOTR. Moreover, they said that the lack of provision in the rules did not render the rules unlawful. AM said this left applicants at the Home Office's discretion with no legal rights, as well as no right to fee waivers. The High Court agreed with the Secretary of State arguments on the legality of the rules saying that 'there is no duty on the Secretary of State, whether in statute or the Rules, to make provision for all such victims and in all circumstances. That must be a matter for the Defendant, exercising her discretion when making the Rules, and not a matter of legal requirement.'[115]

However, it was also argued (with success) that the failure to make provision in the immigration rules for stranded spouses was in breach of Article 14 when read with Article 8 ECHR under the Human Rights Act 1998. It was argued that victims in the UK were given ILR when abandoned, but if they were abandoned abroad they were not given such protection and there was no rational justification for this difference in treatment so it amounted to unlawful discrimination. Counsel for the Secretary of State said that the Home Office was reviewing the policy position but had not reached a decision on what changes if any to make and required time, and furthermore the current situation allowed for her to consider each case individually outside the rules. Lieven J found that these two justifications did not stand up to scrutiny. The Secretary of State had been considering the position for TMA since 2016 without

---

[114] See para. 45

[115] See para. 56

progress. Additionally, it was found that the LOTR process 'severely disadvantage[d] the victims of TMA, in terms of lengthy delay, costs, and the probability that a cohort, of unknown number, may never manage to return to the UK. Further, by having to rely on Leave Outside the Rules, the victims [we]re entirely dependent on the exercise of a discretion with no legal rights, and that discretion seem[ed] to be often poorly understood by Entry Clearance Officers.'[116] The 'impact on the Article 8 family rights of the victims [wa]s therefore very great' and in breach of Article 14 ECHR and the HRA 1998.[117]

It in fact took the Home Office over a year after this judgment was handed down to amend the rules and policy to remedy this breach of the HRA 1998. It can be seen that practitioners needed to think creatively to assist TMA victims to make ILR applications and return to the UK.

5.2 – Appendix VDA and TMA

Fortunately, Appendix VDA, which came into force on 31 January 2024 has remedied this. TMA victims can now apply under Appendix VDA for indefinite leave to enter the UK.

Having set out the important history to this significant change we will now consider how victims can make an application under this route.

As is made clear in Chapter 3, TMA victims must make a valid application for entry clearance from outside the UK; see VDA 1.1-1.4 and 3.1 and 4.3.

Appendix Tuberculosis (TB) does apply to TMA applications; see rule VDA 3.2. This means that 'a valid TB certificate is required if the applicant has been continuously present in a country or countries listed

---

116 See para.76

117 See para. 78

at TB6 for 6 months or more, which includes a period (of any length) within the 6 months before the date of application'; see rule TB2. As hinted at in TB2, there is a long list of countries which require a TB certificate in rule TB6[118]. There is provision for a decision maker to waive the requirement to provide a TB certificate if the individual is unable to obtain the same and it is reasonable to waive the requirement on the facts of the claim; see rule TB5.

We have learnt from Chapter 4, that all applicants under Appendix VDA must meet suitability requirements; see VDA 2.1 and Part 9 of the Immigration Rules. As made clear in Chapter 4, an individual can apply as an overstayer. This is important for TMA victims who will often be left outside the UK close to or after the expiry of their visa for example.

Victims of TMA must have held leave as a partner in the right category (see VDA 4.1(a) to (f)). This is addressed in Chapter 4, too.

The applicant's relationship must have broken down permanently as a result of domestic violence (see VDA 4.2). Again, we have discussed this at length in Chapter 4. However, there are some important differences in assessing this issue in TMA cases, these include the following:

- Significantly, the ADVA Policy accepts that TMA is recognised form of domestic abuse and so this in itself, if accepted, is enough to meet this requirement[119];

- Importantly, the standard of proof for establishing TMA is lower than other DV cases. It is reasonable degree of likelihood as opposed to balance of probabilities. As the ADVA policy says, decisions makers do not need to be certain, convinced or even

118 See also UKVI Guidance on Tuberculosis tests for visa applicants

119 Home Office Policy Guidance Appendix Victim of Domestic Abuse Version 17.0 04 April 2024 p31

satisfied of the truth of the account, it is enough that it can be 'accepted'[120];

- There is an acceptance that TMA victims may not be able to produce evidence in the same manner as victims in the UK. The ADVA Guidance states that if the account is reasonably detailed, consistent and plausible an applicant need not produce medical or independent evidence of DA[121];

- It is also accepted that there can be significant delay in these cases which should not be taken as a credibility issue. It is noted that delay is often owing to TMA, lack of knowledge of rights, isolation, cultural and language barriers, destitution, trauma, mental health issues, and inability to travel[122];

- Cases should be considered for referral to a senior caseworker as a matter of routine[123].

The above shows that a detailed statement addressing for example TMA (how the individual came to travel, what their understanding was at the time of the trip and the length of the same, what arrangements they made for the trip (i.e., time off school and work, return flights, short term holiday letting), what occurred once at the destination, who they have stayed with, when their spouse or partner left, their financial situation, what documents they hold, when they realised they were abandoned, when the relationship ended and whether it ended owing to DV, the circumstances for any children including any separation from them, steps they have taken to return if any, contact with the abuser since they were stranded, attempts to seek advice or obtain their documents, any

---

120 Ibid. p25

121 Ibid.

122 Ibid.

123 Ibid. p26

applications for new documents, when/how realised they could make an application), the history of the relationship, any other DV in the relationship, their immigration history (this is very important), their financial situation if they are applying for a fee waiver, and any difficulties they are facing in obtaining evidence.

Practitioners are advised that if there is other evidence of DV it should be gathered and submitted, as this would inevitably strengthen any application. It may well be that victims of TMA have commenced family court proceedings in respect of children or property so there may well be evidence from the same; see *S (A Child), Re (Guidance in cases of stranded spouses)* [2011] 1 FLR 305 which is discussed above. Practitioners must check whether they have permission to disclose information and documents from such proceedings or they may face serious consequences[124].

As discussed in Chapter 6 dependant children can also apply with their parent or after their parent has applied; see VDA 5.1-8.2.

Where a victim of TMA meets all the above requirements their entry clearance application for settlement will be granted; see VDA 9.1 and 10.1.

If an application is refused, the applicant can challenge an adverse decision by administrative review; see VDA 9.2 and Chapter 7 of this title.

---

124 See for example s12 of the Administration of Justice Act 1960; Rule 12.73 of the Family Procedure Rules 2010; *Nasrullah Mursalin, Re* [2019] EWCA Civ 1559

CHAPTER SIX

CHILDREN AS DEPENDANTS OF VICTIMS OF DOMESTIC ABUSE AND AS VICTIMS OF DOMESTIC ABUSE THEMSELVES

We have already touched upon child dependants of victims of DA being able to apply for settlement under Appendix VDA. We will look at the requirements for children further in this chapter. This chapter also discusses how to assist children when they are victims of domestic abuse themselves.

As explained in chapter 3 of this title, children can apply with their parents or separately from their parents and must make a valid application; see VDA 1.1-1.4.

6.1 – Requirements for a Child Dependant with reference to Appendix Children

With reference to rule VDA 5.1(a)(b) and (c), a dependent child must meet the relationship requirement for settlement, the care requirement, the age and independent life requirement. These matters are to be assessed with reference to Appendix Children. We will work through each of these conditions.

The relationship requirement is set out in Appendix Children.

For the purposes of a VDA application rule, as per CHI 4.1 (a) and (b), the child must be the child of a person (i) who is at the same time being granted settlement on the same route the child is applying on, or (ii) the parent is settled or British and previously had permission on the same route the child is applying on.

As per CHI 4.2 (a), (b) and (d) the child must (i) have last been granted permission as a dependent child of their parent in CHI 4.1, or (ii) have been born in the UK and be applying as a child of the parent in CHI 4.1, or (iii) the child must have been born overseas after the parent's grant of permission as a partner and the child must be applying as a child of the parent in CHI 4.1.

There are obvious problems with CHI 4.2. Consider a family from India for example. The father has refugee status. The children were all born outside of the UK. The children and mother were granted leave under Appendix Family Reunion (Protection). This is leave in line with the father. The father is abusive to the mother and the children and mother flee. The children have not been last granted permission as the dependent child of their mother as per CHI 4.2(a), they were not born in the UK as per CHI 4.2(b), CHI 4.2(c) relates to applications under Appendix UK ancestry and they have not been born overseas after the parent's grant of permission as per CHI 4.2(d). It cannot have been intended that child applicants in this scenario would be excluded intentionally. The children may need to consider other options including seeking LOTR (see Chapter 7).

Usually under CHI 4.3 the child's other parent, who is not the person referred to in CHI 4.1 (c), must be being granted settlement at the same time, be settled or British. However, this does not apply when the child is applying as a dependent child under Appendix VDA (see CHI 4.3(c)).

It is important to note that if the child was born in the UK and they are the child of a person with permission, the child must provide a full UK birth certificate showing the names of their parent(s); see CHI 4.4.

The care requirement is that if the child is under 18, there must be suitable arrangements for the child's care and accommodation in the UK which must comply with relevant UK law; see CHI 2.1.

The care requirement may concern advisers as TMA victims abroad are very unlikely to have accommodation in the UK when they apply. Thankfully, the AVDA Guidance makes clear that this is not a basis of refusal, as victims of TMA and their children can make use of care and support they can seek in the UK as victims of DA[125]. The Home Office Policy Guidance Appendix Children Version 3.0 04 April 2024 states 'If the parent plans to stay with a relative or friend, or to be accommodated with the help of a charity, or in other credible accommodation, you should not refuse the application under the Care requirement unless you have concerns about risk to the child's well-being, beyond not having firm plans'[126].

The age requirement is that the child must be under the age of 18, or they can be over the age of 18 if they were last granted leave to stay as the dependent child of their parent or parents; see CHI 1.1-1.2.

The independent life requirement requires that the child not be leading an independent life; see CHI 1A.1. This means that they do not have a partner (i.e., married or in a relationship akin to marriage which has lasted 2 years or more), and are living with their parent (except where at boarding school, college, university as part of full-time education)[127].

6.2 – English Language Requirements for a Child of a Victim of Domestic Abuse

At the outset it is highlighted that children under the age of 18 are exempt from the English language requirement; see Appendix English Language EL 1.1(b) and 1.2(b).

---

125 Ibid.

126 See p.8

127 Home Office Policy Guidance Appendix Children Version 3.0 04 April 2024, pp7-8

As per VDA 6.1-6.2 a child applicant over the age of 18 must meet an English language requirement and show English language ability on the Common European Framework of Reference for Languages in speaking and listening at level B1 or they must demonstrate that an exemption applies as per Appendix English Language.

Any English Language test must be from an approved provider. These are set out in the UKVI Guidance Prove your English language abilities with a Secure English language test (SELT) updated 28 May 2024. The applicant must provide a valid digital reference number for their test at level B1 or above and it must be dated in the two years prior to the date of application; see EL 6.1.

A child holding a GCSE, an International GCSE, an A level, a Scottish National Qualification at level 4 or 5 or a Scottish Higher or Advanced Higher in English (language or literature) that was awarded by an Ofqual (or SQA, Qualifications Wales or CCEA) regulated awarding body following education undertaken in a UK-based school which began whilst the child was aged under 18 will meet the requirement if this is demonstrated by evidence. The evidence should be either a certificate from the awarding body, or an official transcript issued by the awarding body[128].

Having an academic qualification such as (i) a bachelor's degree master's degree, doctorate awarded in the UK, or (ii) a degree or degree level qualification taught in a university or college in a majority English-speaking country aside from Canada or Ireland, or (iii) a degree or degree level qualification which meets or exceeds the recognised standard of the qualifications listed in (i) above will meet the requirement, so long as the required evidence of the same is provided[129]. Evidence includes (i) a certificate from the awarding body, or (ii) a transcript issued by the university or college that awarded the qualification, or (iii) an official

[128] Appendix English Language EL 7.1-7.2

[129] Ibid. EL 5.2(a-c)

letter from the university or college that awarded the qualification containing information equivalent to a degree certificate, and if the qualification is awarded from a body outside the UK there must be confirmation from Ecctis that the qualification meets the required recognised standard[130].

It must be remembered that an applicant meets the English Language requirement if they a national of a majority English-speaking country as listed out in EL 4.1.

Exemptions from the English language requirement include for example having a physical or mental condition which prevents the individual from meeting the requirement[131].

For further information on the English Language Requirement readers should consider the UKVI Guidance on Assessing the English Language requirement Version 9.0 issued 16 May 2024.

6.3 – Knowledge of life in the UK (KOL UK) requirements for a Child of a Victim of Domestic Abuse

It is also necessary for a dependent child to meet the KOL UK requirements as set out in the immigration rules Appendix KOL UK.

This is demonstrated by the applicant passing the Life in the UK test administered by an educational institution or other person approved for this purpose by the Secretary of State and providing a valid digital

---

130 Ibid. EL 5.3-5.4

131 Appendix English Language EL 1.1(c)

reference number to show this[132]. A Life in the UK Test must be booked through the government website[133].

Again, it must be noted that children under the age of 18 are exempt from the KOL UK requirement; see Appendix KOL UK 3.1(a).

Similarly to the English requirement, exemptions from the KOL UK requirement include for example having a physical or mental condition which makes it unreasonable for the individual to meet the requirement[134].

For further information on the KOL UK requirement those reading should turn to the UKVI Guidance on Knowledge of language and life in the UK Version 28.0 issued 24 November 2022.

6.4 – Maintenance and Accommodation requirements for a Child of a Victim of Domestic Abuse

In addition to the above requirements, a child dependent must show the decision maker there is adequate maintenance and accommodation for themselves without recourse to public funds; see VDA 8.1. This must be shown with reference to the immigration rules set out in Appendix FM-SE: family members specified evidence.

The definition of adequate maintenance is that after tax, national insurance, housing costs (mortgage, rent and council tax), there is available to the family disposable income which meet income support

132 Appendix KOL UK 2.3(a). Please note that there are separate rules for an applicant who was resident in the Isle of Man and the Bailiwick of Guernsey or the Bailiwick of Jersey (see 2.3(b-c)).

133 https://www.lituktestbooking.co.uk/lituk-web/

134 Appendix KOL UK 3.1(c)

levels for a family of their size; see Paragraph 6 of the Immigration Rules[135].

Useful Guidance is provided in the case of *Ahmed (benefits: proof of receipt; evidence) Bangladesh* [2013] UKUT 84 (IAC) on the assessment of adequate maintenance[136]. It is important that benefit rates and assessments are carried out with care[137].

I provide an example assessment of adequate maintenance here for understanding. Mrs S receives working tax credits in the sum of £98 per week. She also receives a weekly net income from cleaning job at £251 per week. Mrs S has two children aged 3, and 7. She resides with a family friend having fled violence and is asked to contribute only £300 a month (£69.23 a week in rent, with no council tax). Her income is £349 a week. Her outgoings on housing costs are £69.23 a week. This as such leave her with £279.77 a week. Income support rates for a lone parent over 18 are £90.50 a week, plus £83.24 for each dependent child (in total £166.48 for the 2 children)[138]. She as such must show a disposable income of £256.98 a week. Looking at the figures her disposable income is at £279.00 a week so her children would meet the requirement.

Immigration advisors must be aware that there is a lengthy definition of 'public funds' in Rule 6 of the Immigration Rules. It states there that 'a person (P) is not to be regarded as having (or potentially having) recourse

---

135 *KA and Others (Adequacy of maintenance) Pakistan* [2006] UKAIT 00065 which held 'The requirement of adequacy is objective. The level of income and other benefits that would be available if the family were drawing income support remains the yardstick.';

Home Office Policy Guidance Part 8 – Family Migration: Adequate Maintenance and Accommodation Version 5.0 08 December 2021, pp 8-9

137 Rightsnet has a very useful poster setting out rates for current and previous years – https://www.rightsnet.org.uk/resources/benefit-tax-credit-rates

138 https://www.rightsnet.org.uk/pdfs/rightsnet-poster-2024-2025.pdf

to public funds merely because P is (or will be) reliant in whole or in part on public funds provided to P's family sponsor unless, as a result of P's presence in the UK, the family sponsor is (or would be) entitled to increased or additional public funds.' This means that where a child is accessing public funds in their own right that may be okay to have regard to in the maintenance assessment, but if a parent is claiming additional public funds owing to the presence of a child this cannot be relied upon.

It is again difficult to see that it was intended that this would be the case. The MVDAC is there to allow for recourse to public funds and when a victim of DA goes on to claim benefits from DWP the amounts the family would be entitled to would have regard to any child who has recourse to public funds. This can then lead to complications with the child dependent meeting maintenance and accommodation requirements. This book is not intended to be welfare benefits advice and applicants may need to consider such advice.

Where children cannot meet the maintenance requirement there may be a need to consider LOTR (see Chapter 7). One also wonders whether there may be a challenge to this rule going forward, given the problems that it causes, the complexities that arise and the purpose of the AVDA rules.

Adequate accommodation must be owned or legally occupied by the family unit. Accommodation can be shared with others. There should be exclusive use of at least the bedrooms required. There should not be overcrowding. This is to be assessed by reference to the Housing Act 1985 with reference to the numbers, age, and genders of those in the household[139].

[139] Home Office Policy Guidance Part 8 – Family Migration: Adequate Maintenance and Accommodation Version 5.0 08 December 2021, Pp 17-21

This title does not address the requirements of Appendix FM-SE in further detail as that would undoubtedly be a book in itself. However, practitioners are asked to consider the rules in full and the Home Office Policy Guidance Part 8 – Family Migration: Adequate Maintenance and Accommodation Version 5.0 08 December 2021.

People reading this book may be worried about this requirement. In particular, there may be concerns in TMA cases about finances and accommodation. Please have regard to the text under 6.1 above and the care requirement, and how prospective support and accommodation will be considered and that the AVDA Guidance makes clear that this is not a basis of refusal.

Those instructed in these cases should also be aware that where this requirement or any of the above requirements cannot be met there is the option under the AVDA Guidance for LOTR to be granted[140]. We will discuss this further in Chapter 7.

It is clear that where children are involved, there must be care in advising as there are several complications which can arise.

6.5 – Children as Victims of Domestic Abuse

As is clear from the above requirements, children are granted under Appendix VDA when their parent is being granted settlement or has settlement under Appendix VDA.

As discussed in Chapter 1 children can be victims of DV in their own right. Helpfully, the Guidance acknowledges children should not be left in an abusive household[141]. Practitioners may come across cases where a child victim of domestic abuse wishes to flee the abuse and apply

140 See page 53

141 Ibid.

themselves, and the parents wish to remain together for example. The AVDA Policy Guidance must be considered in these circumstances. This says that in circumstances where a child applies and the parent has not applied for or been granted settlement, the decision maker should consider granting LOTR with reference to s55 of the Borders Citizenship and Immigration Act 2009[142]. We will look at this further in Chapter 7.

---

142 Home Office Policy Guidance Appendix Victim of Domestic Abuse Version 17.0 04 April 2024 p50

CHAPTER SEVEN

USING POLICY GUIDANCE IN MORE COMPLEX CASES

It can be seen from Chapters 2 to 6 that there will be victims of domestic violence who will not be able to make an application under Appendix VDA and who may not meet the requirements.

It is also important for practitioners to advise on other immigration applications that could be made, for example:

- A protection claim[143];
- A human rights claim based on family (the Applicant may have a child or other close and dependent relationships in the UK so may meet the requirements of Appendix FM or have a strong claim outside the rules) or private life (the Applicant may be able to meet the test under PL 5.1(b) of the Immigration Rules on the basis of very significant obstacles to their integration if returned);
- A human rights claim based on outstanding family court proceedings;

143 See for example *SA (Divorced Women-Illegitimate Child) Bangladesh* [2011] UKUT 00254 (IAC), *KA and Others (domestic violence-risk on return) Pakistan CG* [2010] UKUT 216 (IAC), *BK (Risk-Adultery-PSG) India CG* [2002] UKIAT 03387

- A human rights claim based on health.

This list is not exhaustive.

Importantly, the AVDA Policy Guidance states that 'Leave outside the rules (LOTR) on compelling compassionate grounds may be granted where the decision maker decides that the specific circumstance of the case includes exceptional circumstances. These circumstances will mean that a refusal would result in unjustifiably harsh consequences for the applicant or their family, but which do not render refusal a breach of Article 8 European Convention on Human Rights (ECHR), Article 3 ECHR, Refugee Convention or other obligations'[144]. This definition in itself is quite confusing as immigration practitioners will know that exceptional circumstances and unjustifiably harsh consequences are frequently referred to in the context of Appendix FM and Article 8 ECHR applications; see for example, *Agyarko and Ikuga, R (on the applications of) v Secretary of State for the Home Department* [2017] 1 W.L.R. 823 at §60.

Fortunately, pages 18 and 19 of the AVDA Policy provides examples of circumstances where it would be appropriate to consider a grant of settlement LOTR even where the Applicant does not hold leave as a partner in one of the categories listed in VDA 4.1. This includes:

- Where a TMA victim was granted leave to enter in another category, such as maybe as a parent of a British or settled child or as a visitor, and this was because there was a lack of route of entry for TMA victims at the relevant time;

- Where the abusive partner has subjected the victim to controlling behaviour, which includes preventing the victim of DA from

[144] See p53

being on a partner route to settlement by for example leaving them with leave as a fiancé or a proposed civil partner;

- Where the victim of DV entered the UK in a non-partner route, such as on a visit visa, and the perpetrator of violence has informed the victim they will make an application on their behalf as a partner or tell them that they have made such an application and do not do so leaving the victim liable to removal.

It is clear that this approach will assist many victims who do not meet the eligibility criteria.

The above list however is said not to be exhaustive and there may be other circumstances where it is appropriate to consider LOTR. We have discussed some of the circumstances in this book, for example in relation to child dependants and child victims.

Helpfully, the AVDA Policy also states that 'Not all LOTR is granted for the same reason and discretion is applied in different ways depending on the circumstances of the claim and the applicant's circumstances. There are separate pieces of guidance for deciding cases raising factors relevant to exceptional circumstances, discretionary leave and compelling compassionate grounds'[145]. This highlights the need for individualised consideration and arguments, and for practitioners to be familiar with a range of Policy Guidance documents, such as:

- Family Policy Family life (as a partner or parent) and exceptional circumstances Version 21.0 dated 17 May 2024

- Discretionary Leave Version 10.0 dated 16 March 2023

- Leave Outside the Rules Version 3.0 dated 29 August 2023

[145] Ibid.

The AVDA Guidance requires that where there is a refusal of settlement under AVDA, decision makers should consider, in discussion with a senior caseworker or relevant Home Office team, whether it would be appropriate to grant leave, i.e., permission to stay or settlement outside the rules[146].

This highlights the need for practitioners to advance arguments for LOTR and to challenge decisions where the circumstance are not being considered adequately or at all.

146 Ibid.

CHAPTER EIGHT

CHALLENGING REFUSALS UNDER THE IMMIGRATION RULES AS A VICTIM OF DOMESTIC ABUSE

8.1 – Administrative Review

Any application under Appendix Victim of Domestic Abuse that is refused will come with a right to challenge the decision by way of Administrative Review. The decision notice will inform the applicant of the right to apply for administrative review.

Administrative review is where there is an independent review of the decision by the UKVI (a different person on a different team to the initial decision maker) to see whether the decision was wrong[147].

As per Immigration Rule Appendix Administrative Review AR 1.1 a negative decision under AVDA is eligible for administrative review. It is a decision to refuse an application for permission to stay or entry clearance (see AR 2.1).

Any application for administrative review must be made online on the Administrative Review form which is available on the gov.uk website[148] (AR 2.4).

---

147 Home Office Policy Guidance Administrative Review Version 12.0 03 September 2021, p44

148 https://www.gov.uk/ask-for-a-visa-administrative-review

The fee for administrative review is £80 and it must be paid[149]. An applicant will be exempt from payment if they were exempt from paying the original application fee for the AVDA application, or if as a result of exceptional circumstances they are unable to pay the fee[150]. In the latter situation this would have to be explained and usually supported by evidence of financial circumstances. The administrative review fee is refunded where the application is rejected as invalid or where a decision is made on administrative review to grant leave[151].

Where an applicant is outside the UK the timescale for seeking administrative review is 28 days[152] from the date of receipt of the decision[153]. The timescale for seeking administrative review where an applicant is inside the UK is 14 days[154].

An administrative review is made on the date it is submitted online[155]. An application must be made within the time limits set out in the rules[156]. However, there is scope to accept the application outside the timescales where the decision maker is satisfied that it would be unjust not to waive the time limit and that the application was made as soon as reasonably practicable. This could be for example where a decision was not received in time, or the individual was in hospital. The Home Office

---

149 AR 2.5(a)

150 Home Office Policy Guidance Administrative Review Version 12.0 03 September 2021, pp25-26

151 Ibid. p7 and p27

152 AR 2.6(b)

153 See Articles 8ZA-B of The Immigration (Leave to Enter and Remain) Order 2000 which strictly sets out when decisions are deemed to be received.

154 AR 2.6(c)

155 AR 2.7

156 AR 2.5(b)

Guidance states that the time limit will not be waived unless there is a compelling reason and that forgetting a deadline, problems with a computer, poor availability of a legal advisor, minor illness or caring for someone with such an illness are unlikely to be acceptable reasons.[157]

A child dependent that was included in the AVDA application can of course be included in an application for administrative review[158].

On administrative review the Home Office reviewer will be considering whether the original decision maker's decision is incorrect because (a) there was a failure to apply, or correctly apply, the relevant Immigration Rule, or (b) there was a failure to apply or correctly apply, Policy Guidance[159]. Given the contents of this book on the issues that arise under the rules and policy there may be a lot of scope for challenge to adverse decisions in individual cases. The UKVI Administrative Review Guidance at p46 advises reviewing caseworkers that 'If you find that the original decision maker followed the correct rules and guidance but it is more likely than not that errors were made in applying them, such that the wrong conclusion was reached, you must withdraw this refusal reason. If the application meets all the other requirements of the Immigration Rules, you must overturn the refusal decision and grant leave.'

There is no scope to argue in an administrative review that a victim of DA is entitled to leave on another basis, for example as a parent of a British child or on medical grounds[160] (see Chapter 7 in this regard).

---

[157] Home Office Policy Guidance Administrative Review Version 12.0 03 September 2021, p22

[158] AR 2.11

[159] AR 3.1

[160] AR 3.2

New evidence cannot be submitted on administrative review unless the decision relates to Part 9 of the General Grounds of Refusal in relation to false representation or deception or a previous breach of immigration laws or it relates to a failure to request specified evidence under Paragraph 245AA of the Immigration Rules or to follow the evidential flexibility policy[161]. If the new evidence is admissible the reviewer can contact the applicant for further information to be provided within a reasonable timeframe[162], but if that information is not provided in the relevant timescale the administrative review will be carried out on only the available information and documents[163].

On administrative review the potential outcomes are as follows:

a. the refusal is withdrawn and the application will be reconsidered;

b. the refusal decision is maintained in full on administrative review;

c. the refusal decision remains in force but one or more of the reasons given for refusal are withdrawn;

d. the refusal decision remains in force but different or additional reasons are given for maintaining the decision[164].

If the decision is maintained for different or additional reasons, a further application for administrative review can be made in line with AR 2.8.

Where a decision to refuse is maintained on administrative review, that can be challenged by pre-action letter and thereafter judicial review. We will look at this further below.

---

161 AR 3.3

162 AR 3.4

163 AR 3.5

164 AR 5.1

If the validity requirements of an administrative review application are not met, i.e., the fee has not been paid or it is submitted in the wrong way or it is out of time without good reason, the application will be rejected as invalid and not considered[165].

There can be no removal whilst an administrative review is pending[166]. Where an applicant holds leave, that leave will continue under Section 3C of the Immigration Act 1971 whilst the time limit for making an administrative review has not passed and whilst any administrative review application made in-time remains outstanding.

If an applicant leaves the UK, or signs an administrative review waiver form waiving their right to administrative review or requests their passport be returned to travel outside the UK, any administrative review will be treated as withdrawn[167]. If any new immigration application is made whilst an administrative review is outstanding the administrative review application is treated as withdrawn the day before the new application is submitted[168].

8.2 – Pre-Action and Judicial Review

If the decision is upheld by administrative review, the next step will be to challenge by pre-action letter and thereafter by judicial review.

It has been held that administrative review is an adequate alternative remedy which needs to be invoked prior to proceeding to judicial review; see for example *R (on the application of Prathipati) v Secretary of State for*

165 AR 2.13

166 AR 4.1

167 AR 4.3 and 4.5

168 AR 4.4

the Home Department (discretion – exceptional circumstances) [2018] UKUT 00427 (IAC) at §74.

Applications for judicial review against these decisions are to be lodged in the Upper Tribunal. An application must be made promptly and so that it is received no later than 3 months after the date of decision[169]. Time runs from the date of the administrative review decision. It is important practitioners familiarise themselves with the Procedure Rules and The Administrative Court Judicial Review Guide 2023.

Judicial review is a chapter in itself but practitioners may be assisted by some pointers of grounds to advance. These may include but are not limited to the following:

a. The decision making is unlawful, as it is contrary to the Immigration Rules and Policy Guidance[170]. A detailed consideration of Chapters 3-7 will assist with arguments in this regard.

b. The decision making is based upon a mistake of fact[171].

c. The decision maker has breached the requirements of procedural fairness[172]. This may occur, for example, when the abusive partner has written to the UKVI with their own account of events

---

169 See Rule 28(2) of The Tribunal Procedure (Upper Tribunal) Rules 2008 ('Procedure Rules')

170 See for example *Lumba (WL) v Secretary of State for the Home Department* [2012] 1 AC 245 at §26

171 E.g., *R (Michael) v Governor of HMP Whitemoor* [2020] EWCA Civ 29 [2020] 1 WLR 2524 at §48

172 See for example, *R (Balajigari) v SSHD* [2019] EWCA Civ 673 [2019] 1 WLR 4647 at §70

which has not been put to an applicant but accepted but the UKVI and taken into account in refusing the claim.

d. The decision is irrational, i.e., the way in which the decision is arrived at is unreasonable in that the the decision maker has failed to consider relevant evidence or too much weight was placed on an irrelevant factor[173] and facts and/or the conclusion arrived at is unreasonable[174].

e. The decision maker has failed to give adequate reasons[175].

Remedies in judicial review are a complex topic. Applicants however should be advised that a judicial review will generally result, if successful, in a mandatory order that the decision is to be reconsidered and/or a quashing order in respect of the decision under challenge resulting in reconsideration[176].

8.3 – Right of Appeal

A refusal under AVDA will not attract a right of appeal.

The appeal regime changed dramatically as a result of s.15 the Immigration Act 2014 (IA 2014) which amended Part 5 of the Nationality, Immigration and Asylum Act 2002 (NIAA 2002). Prior to

---

173 See e.g., *R v Secretary of State for Home Affairs, ex p Harrison* (1987) [1997] JR 113, 119-120

174 For example, *(Mackay) v Parole Board* [2019] EWHC 1178 (Admin) at §38

175 *South Bucks District Council v Porter (No 2)* [2004] UKHL 33 [2004] 1 WLR 1953 at §36

176 See for example Section 12 of The Administrative Court Judicial Review Guide 2023.

the IA 2014 refusals of domestic violence settlement applications did attract a right of appeal.

Section 82 of the 2002 Act only allows an individual to appeal a decision which refuses a protection claim, refuses a human rights claim or which revokes protection status.

There has been argument that a refusal of a settlement DV application does amount to a refusal of a human rights claim. This is particularly where human rights have been raised in a cover letter to an application or in evidence submitted with the application. This could occur for example when arguing that an applicant is involved in family court proceedings so Article 6 ECHR is engaged, or where leave is sought on medical grounds raising issues under Articles 3 and 8 ECHR, or where the applicant has a British child in the UK and qualifies for leave on this basis under Appendix FM[177]. Practitioners will note that AVDA decisions generally only address the requirements of the rules and any submissions made in respect of human rights will not be considered. Instead the UKVI generally advise applicants to make a human rights application with the application fee on the correct form.

This issue has been litigated in the Courts and Tribunal.

In *Baihinga (r. 22; human rights appeal: requirements*) [2018] UKUT 00090 (IAC) the Upper Tribunal held that 'the issue of whether a human rights claim has been refused must be judged by reference to the decision said to constitute the refusal.'[178] This was expanded upon in *MY (refusal of human rights claim : Pakistan*) [2020] UKUT 89 (IAC) which held that 'the Secretary of State decides to refuse a human rights claim if she: (i) engages with the claim; and (ii) reaches a decision that neither C nor anyone else who may be affected has a human right which is of such a kind as to entitle C to remain in the United Kingdom (or to be given

---

[177] Home Office Policy Guidance Rights of Appeal Version 15.0 pp10-18

[178] See headnote 3

entry to it) by reason of that right.'[179] The latter decision was upheld by the Court of Appeal in *MY (Pakistan) v Secretary of State for the Home Department* [2022] 1 WLR 238. Accordingly, as the Home Office are not engaging with human rights claims when they are advanced by applicants in AVDA applications there will be no refusal of a human rights claim and as such no appealable decision.

In *AT, R (On the Application Of) v SSHD* [2017] EWHC 2589 (Admin) Kerr J held that there was nothing irrational about removing appeal rights from domestic violence victims as there would clearly be domestic violence claims which would not have any human rights claim to advance. However, he made an obiter comment that in his view it would be wrong to expect a victim of DA to make two applications for leave, one as a human rights claim and one domestic violence, and that this would in fact discriminate against women who bore the brunt of such violence. It was suggested by the Court that the DV application form be amended to include an option to assert that the claim is also a human rights claim. It has been noted however later by the Court of Appeal that this issue was not fully argued before Kerr J and if it had been there would have been consideration of the fact that the UKVI have a one-application-at-a-time policy[180].

Following the decision of Kerr J the application form was in fact never amended. Practitioners will be aware that through statute[181] and the immigration rules[182] that the Secretary of State can and does require a

---

[179] See headnote 3

[180] *MY (Pakistan) v Secretary of State for the Home Department* [2022] 1 WLR 238 at §56

[181] See Section 50 Immigration, Asylum and Nationality Act 2006

[182] See for example Paragraph 34 of the Immigration Rules

particular procedure to be followed to make an application, including using particular forms and paying specific fees[183].

As indicated above the Home Office operate a one-application-at-a-time. In *MY (Pakistan) v Secretary of State for the Home Department* [2021] EWCA Civ 1500 there was an attempt to challenge this policy but a request was made for the Court to reconstitute themselves as a Divisional Court to determine this challenge which could be advanced by way of only judicial review (MY was in fact a statutory appeal). Ultimately the Court decided that they were 'not in a position to determine the lawfulness of the one-application-at-a-time policy, either generally or as applied to the Appellant, on the basis of the pleadings or the evidence before us' as they were not faced with judicial review proceedings [as it was a statutory appeal] and that was not how the case was advanced[184].

This leaves applicants in a difficult predicament, having to make a choice between seeking settlement on the grounds of domestic violence and seeking leave to remain for 30 months of the basis of their family and private life. With the former application, if an applicant applies with leave, once they are refused and any in-time administrative review is refused, the Applicant will be left without leave whilst pursuing any challenge by pre-action or judicial review and as such unable to work or claim benefits. With the latter application, if an applicant applies with leave and if they appeal in-time, their leave (and all benefits that flow) will continue under Section 3C of the Immigration Act 1971 until they are appeal rights exhausted.

It of course remains open, in an appropriate case, for a challenge to be brought to the one at-a-time application policy. Applicants may of course

---

183 See also Shrestha & Anor, R (On the Application Of) v The Secretary of State for the Home Department [2018] EWCA Civ 2810

184 *MY (Pakistan) v Secretary of State for the Home Department* [2021] EWCA Civ 1615 at para. 5

also ask the Secretary of State to exercise discretion[185]. In *MY (Pakistan) v Secretary of State for the Home Department* [2021] EWCA Civ 1500 ultimately the Home Office did consider his human rights application without requiring a formal application. He went on to appeal that decision and his appeal was indeed allowed on human rights grounds[186].

---

185 *Shrestha & Anor, R (On the Application Of) v The Secretary of State for the Home Department* [2018] EWCA Civ 2810 at para. 29

186 UI-2023-000433 – https://tribunalsdecisions.service.gov.uk/utiac/ui-2023-000433

CHAPTER NINE

VICTIMS OF DOMESTIC VIOLENCE UNDER APPENDIX EU

Appendix EU of the Immigration Rules also offers protection, i.e., settled status or pre-settled status, to victims of domestic violence. We have touched upon this in Chapter 4 and will look at this some more here.

It is important to note that Appendix EU is very difficult to read and indeed dealing with Appendix EU would be a separate book. Whilst this chapter attempts to provide an overview of the provisions, the rules are complicated and do required detailed analysis in each case[187].

It was the case that protection was previously only offered to DV victims who were married or in a civil partnership[188]. Unlike under the Immigration Rules, unmarried partners subjected to DV were not protected under the former provisions. Whilst married and civil partners were able to retain rights of residence where relationships broke down owing to violence, unmarried partners were unable to retain rights of

[187] Please note individuals with EUSS Family Permits are not addressed in this Chapter.

[188] See Regulation 10, The Immigration (European Economic Area) Regulations 2016 and the archived immigration rules https://assets.publishing.service.gov.uk/media/5f69b70ee90e077f59f628ce/Immigration_Rules_-_Archive_06-04-2020.pdf

residence; see for example *Singh (EEA, EFMs)* [2021] UKUT 319 (IAC)[189].

In June 2020 Appendix EU was amended so that from 24 August 2020 all family members of an EEA national can seek status/remain eligible for status if their relationship broke down as a result of domestic violence[190].

An EEA national/citizen has a lengthy definition in Appendix EU. It includes

- a person who holds nationality of a country in the EU, Norway, Switzerland, Iceland, Liechtenstein,
- or a naturalised British national who is also an EEA national, and
- a British national who moved to an EU country with the family member and they have come to the UK[191].

Family members of an EEA national have to have formed their relationship with the EEA national and been in the UK before 23.00 GMT on 31 December 2020. Joining family members who formed their relationship with the EEA national before 31 December 2020 but only

---

189 Please note that there has been other litigation about this issue. In 2012 the First-Tier Tribunal Immigration and Asylum Chamber found that an unmarried partner of an EEA national could retain residence rights where the relationship broke down owing to domestic violence – see https://www.ein.org.uk/news/tribunal-finds-unmarried-domestic-violence-survivors-have-eu-law-rights . As Appendix EU has been amended I do not discuss this in any detail in this book.

190 See Statement of Changes in Immigration Rules CP 232, Explanatory Memorandum to the Statement of Changes in Immigration Rules Presented to Parliament on 14 May 2020 (CP 232)

191 See Regulation 9, The Immigration (European Economic Area) Regulations 2016

came to physically join the EEA national after this date, or children born after 31 December 2020 to an EEA citizen living in the UK are included. Family members are defined as including:

- A spouse or civil partner
- children or grandchildren who are under 21
- dependent children or grandchildren who are 21 or over[192]
- dependent parents or grandparents
- unmarried partner (or durable partners)
- other dependent relatives.[193]

Applicants should note that unmarried partners and other dependent relatives are only considered 'family members' under the EU Settlement Scheme if they have or had an EU residence document issued by the UKVI[194].

---

192 I highlight that children under EUSS include children under the age of 21 (as opposed to 18) and over the age of 21 where they are financially dependent on the EEA national; see Annex 1 of Appendix EU 'child'

193 See the definitions in Annex 1 of Appendix EU: EU other EEA and Swiss citizens and family members, of 'family member of a relevant EEA citizen' and 'family member who has retained the right of residence'; see also Home Office Policy Guidance, EU Settlement Scheme: EU, other EEA and Swiss citizens and their family members Version 23.0, dated 4 April 2024, pp81-82

194 See *Batool and others (other family members: EU exit)* [2022] UKUT 00219 (IAC); *Celik (EU exit; marriage; human rights)* [2022] UKUT 00220

It is important to note that EEA citizens who have status under Appendix EU, which is based on their own EEA nationality and their residence in the UK before 31 December 2020, who are subject to DA will not be able to rely on the domestic violence provisions in Appendix EU and in fact do not need to as they have status independent of any abusive family member.

Individuals may not know what status they have under EUSS. Applicants can log into their UKVI online account and enter the details of a document linked to UKVI account, e.g., passport or BRP[195]. This too however is unlikely to tell them the basis of the grant of status as is any letter which conferred status. The best way to check will be through the Subject Access Request[196].

The DA victims that will be approaching you for advice will have pre-settled status under Appendix EU as the family member of an EEA national. Pre-settled status is granted where an individual has lived in the UK for less than 5 years[197]. Where an individual with pre-settled status has lived in the UK continuously for 5 years they qualify for settled status[198].

Whilst, for example, under Appendix FM leave can be cancelled where a relationship is no longer subsisting (because they no longer meet the requirements of the immigration rules[199]), the same does not apply under

---

(IAC) and *Hasanaj and Vasa v Secretary of State for the Home Department* [2024] EWCA 777: Annex 1 of Appendix EU

195 https://www.gov.uk/view-prove-immigration-status

196 https://www.gov.uk/government/publications/requests-for-personal-data-uk-visas-and-immigration/request-personal-information-held-by-uk-visas-and-immigration

197 See for example Appendix EU14 Condition 1(b)

198 See for example Appendix EU 11 Condition 3

199 See Immigration Rule 9.23.1

Appendix EU. UKVI Policy Guidance makes clear that a case can only be referred for curtailment where the person no longer satisfies any of the eligibility requirements under Appendix EU[200].

Although an individual does not need to make an application when their relationship breaks down owing to DV, when they go to apply for settled status they will have to inform the Home Office of the basis on which they qualify. This means they will need to explain their relationship with the EEA national broke down owing to DA and that they are eligible for settled status on the basis of retained rights as a family member[201].

An individual applying under EUSS has to make a valid application[202], using the required application process[203]. When making an application an individual will need to demonstrate their identity and nationality[204]. This can be done with a passport or a biometric residence permit for example, though it is possible for the UKVI to accept alternative evidence of identity where an applicant is unable to obtain or produce the required document due to circumstances beyond their control or compassionate and compelling reasons[205]. They will also have to provide required biometrics[206].

200 Home Office Policy Guidance, Cancellation and curtailment of permission Version 5.0 dated 5 March 2024, pp38-45

201 See for example Appendix EU 11 Condition 3

202 See Appendix EU, EU 9

203 https://www.gov.uk/settled-status-eu-citizens-families/applying-for-settled-status

204 Appendix EU, EU9(b)

205 Home Office Policy Guidance, EU Settlement Scheme: EU, other EEA and Swiss citizens and their family members Version 23.0, dated 4 April 2024, p33, pp63-68

206 Ibid. p34; Appendix EU, EU9(d)

Where validity requirements for an application are not met under Rule EU9 of Appendix EU, an application will be rejected as invalid[207]. Chapter 3 of this book may be useful to refer to on application validity requirements,

Applicants need to demonstrate they are a family member of a EEA national[208]. This can be done for example with a marriage certificate, birth certificates, evidence of cohabitation for unmarried partners, or evidence of dependency[209].

They will also need to provide evidence of the nationality of the EEA national and evidence of their residence[210], though it is recognised in UKVI Policy Guidance that this may be difficult where the relationship has broken down [211].

In order to qualify for status on the grounds of domestic violence a family member needs to ensure they have not broken their continuity of residence through absences[212]. It is important to note that continuity of residence is broken in a range of circumstances including where there is any relevant decision made to deport or exclude the individual. An applicant will also need to ensure they meet the suitability requirements set out in the rules, which encompasses the circumstances where for e.g.,

---

207 Appendix EU, EU10(1); see also Home Office Policy Guidance, EU Settlement Scheme: EU, other EEA and Swiss citizens and their family members Version 23.0, dated 4 April 2024, p55

208 Home Office Policy Guidance, EU Settlement Scheme: EU, other EEA and Swiss citizens and their family members Version 23.0, dated 4 April 2024, p55

209 Ibid. pp118-145

210 Ibid. pp133-139

211 Ibid. pp133-134

212 Ibid. pp162-171; Annex 1 Appendix EU, 'family member who has retained right of residence' and 'continuous qualifying period';

an individual has a criminal conviction or they have given false information or documents in support of an application to UKVI[213].

The individual will also need to show their relationship broke down owing to domestic violence permanently and that they were in the UK when the relevant relationship broke down[214]. The UKVI Policy Guidance makes clear that a flexible and pragmatic approach must be taken when considering whether the relationship broke down as a result of DV. It states the list of evidence set out in the AVDA Guidance is not exhaustive, all evidence must be considered in the round highlighting that neither Appendix EU nor any other immigration rules specify any mandatory evidence, and that length of time that has passed may make it difficult to obtain evidence of DV[215]. In Chapter 4 of this book I set out how domestic violence should be evidenced at length. Readers are referred to 4.2.2 of Chapter 4.

TMA can of course occur to those with pre-settled status too. Where an individual has been abandoned abroad by an abusive relative without their immigration documents they may be able to apply for a EUSS travel permit to enter the UK[216].

Importantly, the UKVI Policy in this area also states that decision makers can make reasonable enquiries (for example with HMRC for DWP or through Home Office records) on behalf of an applicant where they are struggling to demonstrate eligibility, recognising the obstacles they may face[217]. It is important for applicants to explain if they are having

213 See Appendix EU, EU15

214 Appendix EU, EU10(1); see also Home Office Policy Guidance, EU Settlement Scheme: EU, other EEA and Swiss citizens and their family members Version 23.0, dated 4 April 2024, pp208-209

215 Ibid. pp209-210

216 https://www.gov.uk/euss-travel-permit

217 Ibid. p210

difficulty with evidencing their application, why this is the case and what attempts they have made to obtain evidence. They should request that reasonable enquiries are made by UKVI when making the application and provide as much information as possible to assist the Home Office to carry out enquiries.

As stated above, the leave granted under Appendix EU depends on the individual's length of residence. If the applicant has lived here for less than five years continuously they will obtain pre-settled status[218]. Where they have lived here for five years or more they will obtain settled status[219]. The individual will need to demonstrate their length of residence[220]. This might be done for example, through tenancy agreements, utility bills, P60s, pay slips, bank statements, evidence of self-employment, benefits letters, educational certificates or reports[221].

The inability to obtain immediate settlement simply based on DV is clearly a significant difference from AVDA where victims get ILR regardless of length of residence. I have explained in Chapters 2 and 4 that spouses, civil partners and unmarried partners under Appendix EU with pre-settled status as a family member of an EEA national can apply for the MVDA concession and settlement under AVDA. As Chapter 4 sets out though, there are advantages to retaining EU status so it is important these victims get thorough advice.

Practitioners must keep in mind that an individual may be eligible for settled status for different reasons, i.e., for example as a family member of an EEA national, on the basis of retained rights as a family member

---

218 Appendix EU, EU14

219 Appendix EU, EU11-13

220 See Home Office Policy Guidance, EU Settlement Scheme: EU, other EEA and Swiss citizens and their family members Version 23.0, dated 4 April 2024, p84

221 Ibid. pp232-234

(including e.g., based on divorce/termination of a civil partnership[222], death of the EEA national[223]). In addition to children being eligible for settled status on the basis of length of residence, children under the age of 21 may also be eligible for settled status when their parents (one or both) are granted settled status (as such they may qualify for settled status in less than 5 years)[224].

The Home Office website says that applications under EUSS are likely to take up to a month to process, though they can take longer to process for a range of reasons including where they need to request additional information or documents need to be verified or there is a criminal record[225].

Where an application is made under Appendix EU on the grounds of domestic violence and is refused, the decision attracts a right of appeal[226]. This too is a significant difference from AVDA. The decision will give reasons for the refusal and these must be addressed in the appeal. The

222 Home Office Policy Guidance, EU Settlement Scheme: EU, other EEA and Swiss citizens and their family members Version 23.0, dated 4 April 2024, p93

223 Home Office Policy Guidance, EU Settlement Scheme: EU, other EEA and Swiss citizens and their family members Version 23.0, dated 4 April 2024, p203

224 Home Office Policy Guidance, EU Settlement Scheme: EU, other EEA and Swiss citizens and their family members Version 23.0, dated 4 April 2024, p205

225 Home Office Policy Guidance

226 The Immigration (Citizens' Rights Appeals) (EU Exit) Regulations 2020

appeal must be lodged within 14 days after they are sent the notice of decision[227].

There is clearly a lot to consider when making applications on the grounds of DV. It is imperative applicants are properly advised, as the impact upon their rights and entitlements is likely to be great if mistakes are made.

---

227 See Rules 19 and 20 The Tribunal Procedure (First-tier Tribunal) (Immigration and Asylum Chamber) Rules 2014; see also https://www.gov.uk/immigration-asylum-tribunal/appeal-from-within-the-uk

MORE BOOKS BY LAW BRIEF PUBLISHING

A selection of our other titles available now:-

'A Practical Guide to the Independent School Standards – September 2023 Edition' by Sarah McKimm
'A Practical Guide to Estate Administration and Crypto Assets' by Richard Marshall
'A Practical Guide to Managing GDPR Data Subject Access Requests – Second Edition' by Patrick O'Kane
'A Practical Guide to Parental Alienation in Private and Public Law Children Cases' by Sam King QC & Frankie Shama
'Contested Heritage – Removing Art from Land and Historic Buildings' by Richard Harwood QC, Catherine Dobson, David Sawtell
'The Limits of Separate Legal Personality: When Those Running a Company Can Be Held Personally Liable for Losses Caused to Third Parties Outside of the Company' by Dr Mike Wilkinson
'A Practical Guide to Transgender Law' by Robin Moira White & Nicola Newbegin
'A Practical Guide to 'Stranded Spouses' in Family Law' by Mani Singh Basi
'A Practical Guide to Residential Freehold Conveyancing' by Lorraine Richardson
'A Practical Guide to Pensions on Divorce for Lawyers' by Bryan Scant
'A Practical Guide to Challenging Sham Marriage Allegations in Immigration Law' by Priya Solanki
'A Practical Guide to Digital Communications Evidence in Criminal Law' by Sam Willis
'A Practical Guide to Legal Rights in Scotland' by Sarah-Jane Macdonald
'A Practical Guide to New Build Conveyancing' by Paul Sams & Rebecca East
'A Practical Guide to Defending Barristers in Disciplinary Cases' by Marc Beaumont
'A Practical Guide to Inherited Wealth on Divorce' by Hayley Trim
'A Practical Guide to Practice Direction 12J and Domestic Abuse in Private Law Children Proceedings' by Rebecca Cross & Malvika Jaganmohan

'A Practical Guide to Confiscation and Restraint' by Narita Bahra QC, John Carl Townsend, David Winch

'A Practical Guide to the Law of Forests in Scotland' by Philip Buchan

'A Practical Guide to Health and Medical Cases in Immigration Law' by Rebecca Chapman & Miranda Butler

'A Practical Guide to Bad Character Evidence for Criminal Practitioners by Aparna Rao

'A Practical Guide to Extradition Law post-Brexit' by Myles Grandison et al

'A Practical Guide to Hoarding and Mental Health for Housing Lawyers' by Rachel Coyle

'A Practical Guide to Psychiatric Claims in Personal Injury – 2nd Edition' by Liam Ryan

'Stephens on Contractual Indemnities' by Richard Stephens

'A Practical Guide to the EU Succession Regulation' by Richard Frimston

'A Practical Guide to Solicitor and Client Costs – 2nd Edition' by Robin Dunne

'Constructive Dismissal – Practice Pointers and Principles' by Benjimin Burgher

'A Practical Guide to Religion and Belief Discrimination Claims in the Workplace' by Kashif Ali

'A Practical Guide to the Law of Medical Treatment Decisions' by Ben Troke

'Fundamental Dishonesty and QOCS in Personal Injury Proceedings: Law and Practice' by Jake Rowley

'A Practical Guide to the Law in Relation to School Exclusions' by Charlotte Hadfield & Alice de Coverley

'A Practical Guide to Divorce for the Silver Separators' by Karin Walker

'The Right to be Forgotten – The Law and Practical Issues' by Melissa Stock

'A Practical Guide to Planning Law and Rights of Way in National Parks, the Broads and AONBs' by James Maurici QC, James Neill et al

'A Practical Guide to Election Law' by Tom Tabori

'A Practical Guide to the Law in Relation to Surrogacy' by Andrew Powell

'A Practical Guide to Claims Arising from Fatal Accidents – 2nd Edition' by James Patience

'A Practical Guide to the Ownership of Employee Inventions – From Entitlement to Compensation' by James Tumbridge & Ashley Roughton

'A Practical Guide to Asbestos Claims' by Jonathan Owen & Gareth McAloon

'A Practical Guide to Stamp Duty Land Tax in England and Northern Ireland' by Suzanne O'Hara
'A Practical Guide to the Law of Farming Partnerships' by Philip Whitcomb
'Covid-19, Homeworking and the Law – The Essential Guide to Employment and GDPR Issues' by Forbes Solicitors
'Covid-19 and Criminal Law – The Essential Guide' by Ramya Nagesh
'Covid-19 and Family Law in England and Wales – The Essential Guide' by Safda Mahmood
'A Practical Guide to the Law of Unlawful Eviction and Harassment – 2nd Edition' by Stephanie Lovegrove
'Covid-19, Brexit and the Law of Commercial Leases – The Essential Guide' by Mark Shelton
'A Practical Guide to Costs in Personal Injury Claims – 2nd Edition' by Matthew Hoe
'A Practical Guide to the General Data Protection Regulation (GDPR) – 2nd Edition' by Keith Markham
'Ellis on Credit Hire – Sixth Edition' by Aidan Ellis & Tim Kevan
'A Practical Guide to Working with Litigants in Person and McKenzie Friends in Family Cases' by Stuart Barlow
'Protecting Unregistered Brands: A Practical Guide to the Law of Passing Off' by Lorna Brazell
'A Practical Guide to Secondary Liability and Joint Enterprise Post-Jogee' by Joanne Cecil & James Mehigan
'A Practical Guide to the Pre-Action RTA Claims Protocol for Personal Injury Lawyers' by Antonia Ford
'A Practical Guide to Neighbour Disputes and the Law' by Alexander Walsh
'A Practical Guide to Forfeiture of Leases' by Mark Shelton
'A Practical Guide to Coercive Control for Legal Practitioners and Victims' by Rachel Horman
'A Practical Guide to the Law of Driverless Cars – Second Edition' by Alex Glassbrook, Emma Northey & Scarlett Milligan
'A Practical Guide to TOLATA Claims' by Greg Williams
'A Practical Guide to Elderly Law – 2nd Edition' by Justin Patten
'A Practical Guide to Responding to Housing Disrepair and Unfitness Claims' by Iain Wightwick

'A Practical Guide to the Law of Bullying and Harassment in the Workplace' by Philip Hyland

'How to Be a Freelance Solicitor: A Practical Guide to the SRA-Regulated Freelance Solicitor Model' by Paul Bennett

'A Practical Guide to Prison Injury Claims' by Malcolm Johnson

'A Practical Guide to the Small Claims Track – 2nd Edition' by Dominic Bright

'A Practical Guide to Advising Clients at the Police Station' by Colin Stephen McKeown-Beaumont

'A Practical Guide to Antisocial Behaviour Injunctions' by Iain Wightwick

'Practical Mediation: A Guide for Mediators, Advocates, Advisers, Lawyers, and Students in Civil, Commercial, Business, Property, Workplace, and Employment Cases' by Jonathan Dingle with John Sephton

'The Mini-Pupillage Workbook' by David Boyle

'A Practical Guide to Crofting Law' by Brian Inkster

'A Practical Guide to the Law of Domain Names and Cybersquatting' by Andrew Clemson

'A Practical Guide to the Law of Gender Pay Gap Reporting' by Harini Iyengar

'NHS Whistleblowing and the Law' by Joseph England

'Employment Law and the Gig Economy' by Nigel Mackay & Annie Powell

'A Practical Guide to Noise Induced Hearing Loss (NIHL) Claims' by Andrew Mckie, Ian Skeate, Gareth McAloon

'An Introduction to Beauty Negligence Claims – A Practical Guide for the Personal Injury Practitioner' by Greg Almond

'Intercompany Agreements for Transfer Pricing Compliance' by Paul Sutton

'Zen and the Art of Mediation' by Martin Plowman

'A Practical Guide to the SRA Principles, Individual and Law Firm Codes of Conduct 2019 – What Every Law Firm Needs to Know' by Paul Bennett

'A Practical Guide to Adoption for Family Lawyers' by Graham Pegg

'A Practical Guide to Industrial Disease Claims' by Andrew Mckie & Ian Skeate

'A Practical Guide to Conducting a Sheriff Court Proof' by Andrew Stevenson

'A Practical Guide to Vicarious Liability' by Mariel Irvine

'A Practical Guide to Applications for Landlord's Consent and Variation of Leases' by Mark Shelton

'A Practical Guide to Relief from Sanctions Post-Mitchell and Denton' by Peter Causton

www.ingramcontent.com/pod-product-compliance
Lightning Source LLC
LaVergne TN
LVHW022113200926
848481LV00003B/1164

* 9 7 8 1 9 1 3 7 1 5 9 4 6 *